CW00494758

Managing Consultants

How to choose and work with consultants

Igor S. Popovich

CENTURY
BUSINESS

To the People of Yugoslavia

First published 1995
© Igor Popovich 1995
All rights reserved

Igor Popovich has asserted his rights under the Copyright, Designs
and Patents Act, 1988, to be identified as the author of this work.

First published by
Century Ltd
Random House, 20 Vauxhall Bridge Road, London SW1V 2SA

Random House Australia (Pty) Limited
20 Alfred Street, Milsons Point, Sydney
New South Wales 2061, Australia

Random House New Zealand Limited
18 Poland Road, Glenfield
Auckland 10, New Zealand

Random House South Africa (Pty) Limited
PO Box 337, Bergvlei, South Africa

Random House UK Limited Reg. No. 954009

Papers used by Random House UK Limited are natural, recyclable
products made from wood grown in sustainable forests. The
manufacturing processes conform to the environmental regulations of
the country of origin.

ISBN 0 7126 7582 5

Typeset by SX Composing Ltd
Rayleigh, Essex
Printed in England by Clays Ltd, St Ives plc

Contents

Preface

What is this book about?

> And it occurred to me there is no manual that deals with the real business of motorcycle maintenance, the most important aspect of all. Caring about what you are doing is considered either unimportant or taken for granted.
> Robert M. Pirsig, Zen and the Art of Motorcycle Maintenance

Managing Consultants is a book about two types of corporate people – clients and consultants. These two categories are inseparable. Without clients, there would be no consultants; nobody would need their services. Without consultants, many businesses would cease to exist as a consequence of unsolved problems, deteriorating performance and other fatal flaws, unfulfilled needs or unrealised projects.

Why this book?
The major concepts of doing business, between consultants and contractors on one side and clients and customers on the other, have changed significantly in the past couple of decades. It is strange how little attention has been paid to those changes and this aspect of management in general. On the whole, young professionals and managers have a surprisingly superficial knowledge of this important subject. Many not only lack education and experience in a benign guerrilla warfare with consultants, but are also confused and misguided by myths, beliefs, assumptions and perceptions that excessively constrain them and contribute to false expectations.

It isn't uncommon for consultants to teach and guide their clients how to use consultants. This practice obviously puts clients in a dependent position, and while clients benefit to a certain extent, consultants benefit much more. One of the aims of this book is to avoid dependence of that kind and make clients more effective in the managing process.

This book is not an attack on consultants. It is simply a guerrilla manual for clients who use consulting services. It teaches how consultants operate, how they solve problems and perform various tasks. It also teaches clients how to get the most for their money, how to select the right consultant, how to communicate effectively with them, how to monitor and control their progress, and how to implement their solutions.

Who will benefit from this book?

Many types of client will be able to benefit from the book. Small companies who never or very rarely use consultants because they can't afford their fees; medium and large companies whose use of consulting services is limited, due to budget restrictions, policies or fear of the unknown or rip-offs; and companies, large and small, who regularly use consultants and quite often suffer from unnecessary or excessive consulting, which results in high costs and reduced profits.

The main aim of this book is to make life easier for anybody who uses consulting services – engineers, accountants and other professionals; project managers; personnel, operations, construction and other middle and top managers; small business owners and entrepreneurs.

How can you benefit from this book?

Some managers feel they have to own, oversee and run every activity, every aspect of the business under their control. They have a motto: 'If something is worth doing, I do it myself!' or, 'If I want it done properly, I have to do it myself.' I hope those amongst you who recognise yourselves in these lines will also benefit from this book. Consultants are not bad *per se*. If properly managed, they can be an asset and a great help to any business in need.

Managers' lives will be easier because by using consultants successfully, their jobs will be done on time and within budget, their goals will be reached and their performance, image and status will improve, along with their chances for promotion.

Learning from the experience of others is a very wise policy. This book is a first step in that direction. It won't keep the mistakes away, but if advice given here is followed, it should keep them to an acceptable level.

Most of the principles, strategies and tactics outlined within these covers are also applicable in other aspects of corporate life. They simply teach you how to get the most out of people working for you or with you. Think about them, adopt them and adapt them to suit your way of thinking and your *modus operandi*.

Warning: This book may give you an unfair advantage over your rivals, the internal ones (peers, subordinates, superiors) and the outside ones (opposition, competitors). By managing consultants better, by making sure they work *for you*, not *against you* as happens in some cases, and by joining forces with them through a synergetic relationship, you may significantly improve your own productivity, expertise, status and chances of promotion and success.

If you are afraid of being successful, don't read this book. If you like the challenge and the change, do.

A *matter of gender*

Throughout the book I have used mainly masculine gender. Personally, I dislike using his/hers, he/she and other awkward combinations just to keep equal opportunity puritans happy. Please accept that *he* means both *he* and *she* in this book.

Smart Move
Be critical about this book. Read it creatively and aggressively, with a red pen. Strike out things you don't agree with, underline or highlight parts you find useful. Make dog's ears, stick in notes and write your own ideas on the margins.

The structure of this book

❑ Chapter 1, 'Consultants – Who They Are and How They Work', explains the basics of the consulting profession. It tells you how consultants operate, what types of people become consultants, how they find clients and market their services. It also analyses the benefits and advantages of using consultants and compares them with some disadvantages. Every client has some fears about employing consultants. The causes of those fears and the ways of overcoming them are also looked at.

❑ Chapter 2, 'Selecting Consultants', deals with the first step in every consulting assignment – finding and engaging a suitable consultant. It will teach you how to interview consultants, what questions to ask, how to check their references, how to compare proposals and quotes and how to establish your own database of consultants.

❑ Chapter 3, 'Management of Consulting Projects', starts with a general overview of project management. The seven consulting steps are analysed, followed by the overview of various types of documents clients and consultants produce. Financial issues such as consulting fees, methods of payment, variations and cost control are also dealt with in detail. At the end, a detailed project checklist is given to help you keep track of the major steps in your future projects.

❑ Chapter 4, 'Monitoring and Controlling Consultants', focuses on two methods of control, feedback and feed forward. It shows you what to do when things don't progress the way they should, and how to do it. Some tactics for avoiding pitfalls and expensive mistakes are also given, followed by ways of keeping a constant control over consultants.

❏ Chapter 5, 'Communicating For Success', focuses on two main aspects of communication: active listening and briefing consultants; and negotiating fees and terms of contracts. Some useful hints for effective progress meetings and expressing your views are also covered.

❏ Chapter 6, 'Focus On Clients', starts with client self-analysis. This section helps you understand your strengths and weaknesses by evaluating your personality, previous projects and consultant management experience. You'll not only discover the sixteen most common mistakes clients make, but will also learn about twelve well-known but often forgotten recipes for success in dealing with consultants.

A matter of value

The true value of a book like this one is not in its contents, in my views, suggestions and advice. It is in what you, the reader, learn from it, take out of it and apply in your everyday life. Without application, you won't achieve anything. That would be like learning how to speak effectively without practising giving speeches, or learning how to ride a bicycle without getting on it.

The key word that applies to any self-improvement book is ACTION! Don't merely read this book. Extract the ideas and tactics you like, modify them to suit your circumstances and apply them in your life. Put your knowledge into action!

The principles outlined here are not theoretical, untested concepts. They've been proven by engineers, managers, supervisors. They work in large companies, small firms and for individuals. Some of them are from my own experience in managing projects and dealing with engineering consultants and contractors. All of them have been chosen for their simplicity, practicality and applicability. They should give you the insight and the motivation to apply them to your dealings with consultants.

My hope is that this book will help both clients and consultants to accomplish more, in a shorter time, for less money and with mutual satisfaction.

Igor S. Popovich

Perth, Australia
November 1994

Introduction

The birth of the consulting profession

> *Management consulting is an advisory service contracted for and provided to organisations by specially trained and qualified persons who assist, in an objective and independent manner, the client organisation to identify management problems, recommend solutions to those problems and help, when requested, in the implementation of solutions.*
>
> Larry Greiner and Robert Metzger, *Consulting to Management*

All successful companies are alike. Every unsuccessful company is unsuccessful in a different way. Edwin G. Booz was one of the first to recognise the fact that both successful and less successful companies would pay hefty fees for advice on how to solve their business problems and improve their operations.

Although he was a psychologist by training, he established his firm under the name Edwin G. Booz Engineering Surveys. In those early days, the term 'management consultant' didn't exist and most of the work was in fact time and motion studies. As a direct consequence of Frederick Taylor's ideas, efficiency had become the buzzword, and Booz had 'efficiency experts' working on how to shorten the time needed to perform various labouring tasks. That was called 'scientific management'. The scope of their services gradually expanded into personnel management and recruiting, accounting, marketing, operations research. When Booz died in 1951, Booz, Allen & Hamilton was one of the most respected consulting companies.

The legacy of the name
The difficulty in writing a book on consultants is the broadness of the term itself. A consultant may be an unemployed professional whose ego dictates that he proclaims himself a 'consultant in between assignments' or a retired executive who freelances to whoever wants him. There are consultants whose clients are companies – consulting engineers, architects, management consultants, accountants, lawyers, advertising and marketing agents. There are also consultants who deal with

individuals – career counsellors, psychiatrists, tutors, trainers, sex therapists.

There are even 'stress management' consultants, 'dress for success' consultants and 'leisure' consultants. There are consultants providing information and advice on any human activity imaginable. In this book, a consultant is defined as any individual, group or company who, based on their knowledge and expertise, provides services, advice or guidance of a professional or semi-professional nature to clients and customers.

The term itself is often used as a euphemism for unemployed professionals and managers, who are 'in between jobs'. It sometimes serves as a means to keep executives, who would otherwise have to retire, on their companies' payroll lists.

Consulting in a nutshell

Consulting provides quick access to expertise in times of need, allows flexibility in hiring and operating, and usually produces quite satisfying results. It also comes in a range of sizes, costs, methods, principles, practices, levels and philosophies, to cater for any need imaginable.

Experiences with consultants vary from client to client. Some clients form lasting business relationships which benefit both sides, others burn their fingers on unsuccessful projects. Almost everyone has either had his own bad experience with consultants, or has heard about someone who has.

The costs of those failures are usually significant, not only from the financial point of view, but also tarnishing the image of the consulting profession as a whole. The only professions with worse reputations are lawyers (who may be classified as a special breed of consultant), used-car salesmen and estate agents.

Unfortunately, the best consultants on any issue are not employed as consultants. They either drive taxis or work in hair salons.

The McKinsey Way

James O. McKinsey (1889-1937), an economics professor at the University of Chicago, founded his consulting firm in 1926. He wrote numerous articles and four books. One of them, *Budgetary Control*, was the first definitive book on budgeting. The book helped him to secure business, most of which came from banks and other financial institutions.

After successfully completing a project for Marshall Field & Co., he became chairman and chief exeuctive officer of McKinsey and Co. In 1937 he contracted pneumonia and died at the age of forty-eight. His partners kept the business running and made it into one of the biggest and most respectable consulting houses.

Consulting, and especially management consulting, in its essence deals with 'people' problems, because most business problems are people problems. Each consultant is, in a way, an unlicensed psychiatrist. He's someone a manager can turn to and confide in. Most managers are very lonely and isolated from other employees, even from their assistants and peers.

Consulting is a multifaceted business. It is a basket which contains many different disciplines, such as contract law, recruitment and selection, project management, communication, budgeting, forecasting and tendering. There is no such thing as a typical consultant. Due to that fact, it is hard to generalise and find the common denominators that are shared by most consultants. Nevertheless, this book will attempt to pinpoint those common denominators for you.

The information contained in this book is based on the views and opinions of the author. Legal and professional advice should always be obtained where necessary.

Chapter 1: Consultants – Who they are and how they work

The Basics

There's no business like consulting business

> *They [management consultants] are people who borrow your watch to tell you what time it is and then walk off with it.*
> R. Townsend, *Up the Organization*

Consulting organisations are collections of people, working together to provide services to their client organisations, with one basic purpose – to help them achieve goals they could not reach without outside assistance.

Consulting as a business venture has low overheads and requires low capital start-up investment. This makes it easier for consulting firms to adapt to changes relatively quickly, and to position themselves differently should a fresh marketing approach or a new image creation be necessary.

The intangible nature of the consulting business also brings associated disadvantages. Services, as compared to products, cannot be stored and sold later, when boom replaces bust, and the management of a consultancy firm is a factor crucial to its profitability.

Individuals working for consulting companies could be classified as knowledge workers. They are professionally trained to analyse information and process it into studies, reports, designs, plans and budgets. Most of those activities are performed in their offices, at desks, using pen and paper, calculator, drawing board and personal computer.

Irrespective of their age, education, experience, specialisation, company size, industry or location, they generally perform similar problem-solving work, day in, day out. They are troubleshooters, designers, planners, analysts, systems specialists, auditors, project managers, recruiters, efficiency experts, programmers.

Consulting is not recession-proof

> *All of this reinforces the idea that consulting practices are less like farming and more like fishing. In farming you plant a crop, tend it, and it grows, the same way most businesses work. With fishing, you have to work at it all the time and there is no natural growth. In farming, if the soil is weak you can fertilise. In fishing, if there aren't any fish, you have to move to another place.*
>
> Carl D. Peterson, *Staying in Demand*

The preconceived notion that consultants get called in when times are tough, when businesses are unhealthy and when there is a problem to be solved is only partially true. A comparison that portrays consultants as doctors for making sick companies healthy is even less accurate. The better analogy would be to call them health, wellbeing, fitness and nutrition advisers. Many clients are relatively healthy companies.

Consulting is a knowledge-based, service-orientated business, which has relatively low overheads. These overheads include office costs (rent, heating, cleaning, electricity, furniture and decor), secretarial services (typing, copying, drafting, binding, desktop publishing, telephone and fax), administrative services (accounting), staff training costs and insurance (office and equipment, public liability, etc.).

Despite the fact that consulting is a labour-intensive business, providing there is a healthy backlog of assignments, profit margins can be quite large, due to the relatively high fees clients are charged. However, once new assignments stop coming in, there isn't enough work for every staff member and in many cases staff numbers are simply reduced to keep the whole operation profitable.

Consulting is not recession-proof. In terms of vulnerability, it could be compared to the training industry. Although every manager recognises the importance of effective and relevant training and the need for developing employees, the first cost that is usually slashed when things start to go wrong is the training bill. Consulting costs share the same fate. It's a simple matter of economics.

Mental exercise
Which business are consultants in?
a) The consulting business
b) The problem-solving business
c) The knowledge-selling business
d) The fee-maximising business

The changing role of the consulting profession

There are very few professions that are changing as much as consulting is. Clients and consultants are constantly finding new and innovative ways of doing business and increasing the benefits that flow to both sides in the consulting process.

The main change that has occurred is in the role of the consultant itself. In the old days consultants would advise and make recommendations. In the last few years, clients have started to want solutions and working systems, not just recommendations. Today's consultants must be able to offer packaged deals and turnkey solutions.

Employers are facing two major challenges. The first is downsizing and outsourcing. Companies are refocusing on their core activities and outsourcing all others. They are also cutting back the number of employees and expecting the remaining ones to perform various duties and learn new skills. The second push from the employers is towards cost-cutting and profit maximisation through better and more effective use of outside consultants and contractors. In an attempt to avoid parting with hard cash, many clients are looking for alternative methods of payment and are offering consultants profit-sharing deals and schemes of various kinds.

Clients are also becoming focused on the bottom line. They want to know beforehand what specific and tangible benefits each consulting assignment will bring and how those benefits are going to affect their business and profits.

The attitude of individual employees towards consultants has also changed dramatically. In past decades employees feared for their jobs. Today they welcome the outside help and the subsequent reduction in their own workload.

Consultants have also changed their approach to finding clients, by using novel and creative ways of generating new business. They are responding to changing clients' needs and offering more practical and profitable solutions than ever before.

Where do consultants learn to be so smart?

> 'And how many hours a day did you do lessons?' said Alice, in a hurry to change the subject.
> 'Ten hours the first day,' said the Mock Turtle, 'nine the next, and so on.'
> 'What a curious plan!' exclaimed Alice.
> 'That's the reason they're called lessons,' the Gryphon remarked: 'because they lessen from day to day.'
> Lewis Carroll, Alice's Adventures in Wonderland

There is no formal education in consulting, and even training courses for hopefuls who would like to join the ranks of 'the chosen ones' are very rare, almost nonexistent. Just as full-time employees learn and develop their skills on the job, consultants learn and practice while working for their clients. In a sense, clients pay them to learn.

A university degree is considered a prerequisite for entering the consulting profession. Many employees of consulting firms have two degrees or hold an MBA, which is still perceived as a ticket to prestigious jobs, despite its limitations and narrow focus on quantitative management methods. Just as engineering schools assume that everybody will work in a research and development centre, or at least in a design office, business schools indoctrinate consultants to believe that they'll spend most of their time managing, supervising and controlling, rather than doing specialist, very often detailed or even tedious and monotonous work based on their know-how and experience.

Although most consultants have a specialist training in disciplines such as engineering, law, accounting or economics, they also have to develop broad, so-called generalist skills. They must be able to think rationally, to evaluate, communicate, solve problems and understand the complexities of systems, organisations and markets. This duality is the trademark of a successful consultant. He must be a true professional and a specialist in a certain discipline, yet also a writer, trainer, troubleshooter, speaker, negotiator and anything that the consulting business requires him to be. For independent freelancers, business skills are also necessary, for they are responsible for running their own practices.

The almighty Pareto principle, better known as the 80/20 rule, can be applied liberally to a consultant's education. No matter what his background is, in accounting, law, engineering or the humanities, 80 per cent of what he was taught at university won't be used in practice. Furthermore, it can be postulated that 80 per cent of the knowledge that a consultant will need on the job won't be taught through formal education.

Most consulting work is basically glorified information-gathering and data analysis. It usually takes far too long and costs far too much for what it's really worth.

Consultants are generally better informed than their clients are. They do more trade, professional and general reading, they attend more seminars, meetings and presentations. So, one of the obvious ways for a client to correct that imbalance in power is to cut down or completely eliminate time-wasting activities and substitute them with reading and gaining some hands-on experience.

> **The One-minute Manager**
> Are you a famous 'one-minute' manager? Do you spend one minute managing and the rest of your work day wasting time? If so, that is exactly the reason why your consultant knows more than you do, and, consequently, earns more than you do.

Why people become consultants

❑ *Fear of losing their jobs.* Many competent people suffer from a fear very common amongst professionals – a fear of losing their jobs. The reasons vary: restructuring, mergers, plant closures, downsizing, bankruptcies, forced retirement, etc. They simply cannot wait for the axe to fall, so they actively search for opportunities as freelance consultants or look for employment with established consulting firms.

❑ *Feeling underpaid and underutilised.* Some people with valuable knowledge, skills and experience feel grossly underpaid, and what is even more important, underutilised. Their employers either don't see their capability or don't know how to deploy them for maximum benefit. Consulting is an ideal pressure outlet. They have what it takes, so why not make the best of it and get paid what they are really worth?

❑ *Compulsory retirement comes too early for many active and industrious employees.* They simply don't want to stop working, they are fired for action. For many people age is not the problem, it is the fear of becoming idle, passive, obsolete, unwanted. They feel that once that spark of ambition and enthusiasm that drives them is extinguished, their lives will not be worth living. Their experience, business contacts and reputation make them ideal for the consulting profession.

❑ *Entrepreneurial spirit.* This is one of the major reasons for becoming a consultant. Many solo fliers realise that working for someone else will not make them rich and that being one's own boss, calling the shots and shaping one's own destiny is a much better option. Compared to other businesses, where start-up costs run into hundreds of thousands of pounds, setting up a one-person consultancy doesn't even require an office; many start in the spare bedroom. It only requires stationery, business cards, a telephone, a fax machine and a personal computer. And, of course, clients.

❑ *The very nature of consulting life appeals to some people.* They are attracted by the dynamic, ever-changing and challenging environment, by daily interaction with clients, by the fact that consulting can be enjoyable and a source of great fun. They are thrill-seekers.

❑ *'Thankless' organisations.* To many employees, 'modern' organisations are as modern as the Catholic Church or the French Légion d'honneur. So-called 'contemporary' organisations are not contemporary at all. They are still based on the same premises they were based on twenty or forty years ago.

Despite the wishes and hopes of management, some companies are so inhuman and demeaning that many idealistic employees feel out of place. Their eyes are set on the blue skies above, but their wings are constantly trimmed. They quickly become dissatisfied with the lack of creativity, challenge, opportunity for professional or personal growth and, above all, with the lack of human touch and genuine interest in employees.

❑ *Consulting is a short cut to top management positions.* An ambitious consultant liaises with senior management on a regular basis, while working on important problems in which those managers have a direct and personal interest. This will make him known and will establish bonds with his clients, so that next time those managers need a professional to fill some permanent senior position, the choice will be obvious.

What kind of people do consulting companies want to employ?

It requires a very unusual mind to make an analysis of the obvious.
A. N. Whitehead

First of all, consultancies, like all other employers, prefer candidates who are already in employment. They want ambitious people who are looking for better, more challenging and rewarding careers, not people who don't even have a job.

They look for independent thinkers with well-developed reasoning ability, though not too independent, as this would make it difficult for individuals to accept and adapt to either the firm's culture and values or those of its clients.

Being a self-starter is a definite requirement, as is the ability to work efficiently in a team environment. These may sound like opposing qualities, but they reflect another duality of the consulting profession. Freelance consultants work alone most of the time.

Loneliness is one of the consultant's biggest problems. This is especially so for freelancers. They don't belong to the organisation. They are outsiders. As employees of consulting firms, consultants are more likely to work as members of a team.

Controlled aggression and the ability to handle a client's negative or hostile reactions with calm and composure are amongst the most valued psychological traits of potential candidates.

A 'multitasking mind' – the rare ability to keep all aspects of a problem or an issue in one's mind at the same time – is an extremely valuable quality, particularly at more senior levels, where assignments are complex and issues clouded.

Candidates also have to be able to operate comfortably in unknown environments and have the capacity and personality to quickly develop productive and comfortable relationships with clients and other members of a project team.

Bimodal thinking is another quality of top consultants, who are able to deal with both macro and micro issues. Analysing problems and issues within a client's organisation requires broad, macro views, while the application of solutions calls for a micro approach, with attention to detail.

It has been said that the consultant's job is to see possibilities and opportunities before they become obvious to clients and then to explore those possibilities. That talent is certainly an asset for an individual, especially for management consultants.

Systems thinking – the ability to comprehend the whole, not just the parts, and the ability to integrate goals, ideas and requirements into an overall plan or concept – is a quality of paramount importance, the very one that is sadly lacking in many consultants at the bottom of consulting firms' hierarchies.

All of the traits mentioned so far can make a consultant, but they can't make a good consultant. The quality that makes a good consultant is intellectual honesty. This means telling clients the truth, even if the truth hurts. It also means putting clients' interests first and doing one's best to deliver what was promised, even if that means loss of profits, uncompensated overtime and sleepless nights.

Who is who in a consulting company?

> *Every successful enterprise requires three men – a dreamer, a businessman, and a son-of-a-bitch.*
>
> Peter McArthur

There are two basic approaches consulting companies use to get an assignment. The first one is a specialist's approach. Their message reads: 'You people need some help in this area, which happens to be our speciality. We can do all these wonderful things for you and solve your particular problem.'

The other approach is used by generalists, the multidisciplinary practices who can deal with various aspects of management, accounting, engineering, law, or whatever their niche is. They say: 'We can help you restructure your business, streamline it, make it more effective and profitable. Our broad experience base and system integration approach to problem-solving will not only make sure the issues are addressed individually, but we'll also look at how those issues relate to each other and how you can organise and position yourselves to maximise your strong points and neutralise your weaknesses.'

As in any organisation, consulting companies employ people with different personalities, of various backgrounds and experience, whose roles are different from each other. Formally, they all do the same tasks, so those differences often go unnoticed by clients, but behind the scenes their personalities surface and each acts as a cog in a smoothly ticking (well, most of the time) consultancy machine.

❑ *The Rainmaker*. He's an ambassador. He travels, keeps in touch with clients and, most importantly, brings the business in. He's a figurehead, a symbol of the firm. His task is to keep up the firm's reputation and appearances. The only problem is that he doesn't do any consulting. He's just bait for attracting clients' attention. The actual work is done by others. His second task is to create the right kind of atmosphere in which the maverick, the brainstormer and others can work to the best of their abilities.

❑ *The Spokesman*. He's the negotiating arm of the firm. Usuallly a lawyer, his legal background gives him a strategic advantage in dealing with client firms, whose managers in most cases aren't lawyers. Being outspoken and articulate, rhetoric is his cup of tea. He conducts reviews and meetings and is responsible for smoothing the rough edges when things aren't progressing as planned.

❑ *The Maverick*. He's the leader of the project team, the engine that keeps the consulting machine moving. His drive, enthusiasm, persistence, resilience and tenacity keep projects from stalling or sidetracking. Usually, the most experienced and trusted member of the consulting team. He reports directly to the rainmaker, and is personally responsible for the whole assignment. He's the dynamo, the one who makes progress and makes sure the deadlines are met.

❑ *The Analyst*. His task is to analyse and disseminate ideas, proposals and concepts, because this is exactly what clients do when evaluating consultants' work. The analyst serves as an internal quality controller, who puts to the test anything that goes out to clients. His main task is to pick up flaws, omissions, errors, inconsistencies, fallacies and other potentially harmful or embarrassing imperfections.

❑ *The Brainstormer*. Brainstorming is a creative, intuitive and imaginative activity. The brainstormer is a creative think-tank. His task is to come up with new, more efficient and unorthodox ideas. Some call him the devil's advocate. He is the outsider who challenges the insiders' way of thinking, the one who brings in fresh approaches and unbiased views.

❑ *The Organiser*. In hospitals they call them matrons. In police stations, sergeants are the equivalent, because this is what the organiser does – organises. People, resources, time, clients, meetings, projects.

❑ *The Detailer*. His main tool is a fine-toothed comb, with which he sifts through contracts, designs, drawings, reports, recommendations, correspondence and other deliverables to clients. His main task is to make sure everything is right, down to the finest detail.

People who are good at mastering concepts, ideas and trends usually aren't very thorough when details are in question. Many clients, on the other hand, either intentionally or unintentionally, pay special attention to small things, which can spoil the big picture. A shrewd consulting company knows that and will employ a detailer who makes sure nothing is left to chance.

❑ *The Concept Man*. He is the visionary, the ideas man who lives in a world beyond trivialities and technicalities. He produces concepts, notions and ideas to be further evaluated, elaborated upon and applied by the analyst, maverick and detailer. Then they are sold to clients by the rainmaker and spokesman.

❑ *The Prostitute*. This character doesn't care what he does, as long as the rewards are substantial. For him, there are no unpleasant, unethical, immoral or improper tasks, just well-paid and poorly paid assignments. He prefers the well-paid ones. He usually gets the less glamorous tasks, the ones everybody else in the firm shies away from. Although officially the prostitute operates behind the scenes, far from the inquisitive clients' eyes, he holds an important position. Managers like people who will do the dirty washing for them, and consulting firms are no exception.

❑ *The Foot Soldier*. Member of the 'elite' consulting troops. He interviews employees, customers and competitors, gathers and sorts tons of information, prepares data tables, charts and graphs, checks drawings, plans and previous studies. He is the bee who brings pollen into a consulting beehive, to be processed and fermented into sweet, sticky honey to feed the hungry clients.

❑ *The Freelancer*. The term 'free lance' originated in medieval times. Knights who were in no permanent personal service to kings, lords or other feudal aristocracy set their lances for hire. They would fight for anyone who paid the requested price. These mercenaries owed no permanent allegiance to anyone and were free to choose who they wanted to work for and how they wanted to live their lives. These days the freelancer operates mainly as an independent consultant, but he also often subcontracts to other consulting firms.

❏ *Support staff.* Office work in a consulting company doesn't differ much from that in other service orientated companies. The clerical and secretarial staff handle typing, note-taking, in-house publishing (printing, binding, photocopying) and other standard administrative duties. Accounting staff take care of accounts payable, accounts receivable, payroll, etc. Regardless of their title, their main task is to support the professional consultants, so that they can function with the utmost efficiency and profitability for the firm.

The life cycle of a consultant

There are three general types of consultancy. Some have a policy of recruiting young college graduates or MBAs and grooming them for years, until they are ready to take top positions. Others tend to build their practices by attracting outstanding individuals from other consultancies or, sometimes, from their clients' companies. The majority use a mixture of these two methods.

Typically, young graduates begin their career as 'foot soldiers' – officially, junior consultants – who assist senior consultants and grow in the process. They learn quickly and, being impressionable and easily indoctrinated, soon adopt the firm's values and methods.

Most prominent firms have a career path system which gives professionals scope for personal development. In McKinsey they call it 'up or out'. It is based on a progression of gradually increasing responsibility through the successful completion of more and more difficult and challenging assignments. Those who achieve results fit well into the scheme; those who don't have no future in the firm.

As individuals become seasoned consultants, their titles change from just 'consultant' to senior consultant, partner and senior partner. It goes without saying that consulting firms invest heavily in further training. Again, some firms use a battery of formal training courses spanning three, six or even twelve months, while others send consultants out in the field much sooner than that, under the guidance of experienced professionals. Regardless of the policy, a new recruit isn't fully productive for quite a long time. Most consulting firms claim that it takes them two to three years to recover the costs of training and to start making profits once the young guns begin to earn their keep.

The tangible aspects of the consulting business

Clients

Consulting is a service business, and as such it is naturally strongly client-orientated. A client is the consultant's customer, the consumer of his products – knowledge, advice, studies, proposals, surveys, designs, construction and engineering projects, or anything else for that matter.

The key to a mutually beneficial relationship lies with the client. The balance of power is slightly tilted in his favour. He needs the consultant, because he has problems which, due to lack of knowledge or time, he can't solve himself. But the consultant needs the client even more, because his very existence depends on his clients. Without a steady flow of work, he would have to reduce staff levels and ultimately close the business. In a sense, the client's misfortune is the consultant's fortune. Lawyers and doctors belong to the same group of service providers. Healthy, happy people without problems generally don't need doctors, lawyers or consultants.

The pace of doing business has increased dramatically in the last decade. Both client and consultant may be busy at times. However, no matter how busy the consultant is, it is the client who should set the time frame. It would not be appropriate for a consultant to dictate when he intends to respond to a client's requests. It is his responsibility to adjust his schedule in order to accommodate his client's requests and to respond within limits set by the client.

It is important to remember that clients are:

❑ the most important people to a consultant
❑ not dependent on consultants: the opposite is true
❑ doing consultants a favour by dealing with them: the opposite is not true
❑ not outsiders to a consultant's business, but part of it
❑ not a nuisance or interruption to a consultants' work, but the source and purpose of it

What sort of problems can consultants solve?

> The real problem is what to do with the problem solvers after the problems are solved.
>
> Guy Talese

Your success as a professional or a manager depends heavily on your ability to achieve results. In most cases, those results will be achieved by other people, including consultants, to whom you delegate tasks and who can help you reach your predetermined goals. Managing is the art of delegation.

To make your life easier and your success more likely, you have to recognise and hire talented people. You can hire them on a permanent basis, as your employees, or an on *ad hoc* basis, as consultants.

The most common problems keeping organisations and individuals from getting what they want can be summarised in the following categories:

❑ *Lack of funds*. Money problems. Liquidity and cash-flow problems.

❑ *Lack of expertise*. Insufficient technical knowledge about a product or a system.

❑ *Lack of communication*. Poor management of people. Barriers, groups and rivalry.

❑ *Lack of time*. Poor time-management skills. Poor planning and controlling.

❑ *Lack of human resources*. Not enough skilled and competent people. Lack of experience or education.

❑ *Lack of information*. Poor data-gathering and fact-finding skills.

❑ *Lack of organised and planned effort*. Goals are not clearly defined or communicated, maybe even nonexistent.

❑ *Lack of positive spirit, belief in the individual and group values and goals*. Bad organisational spirit. Poor motivation. Negative attitudes. Fear of the unknown, of success or failure.

Why Clients Hire Consultants
To learn
To save money
To avoid losses
To solve problems
To improve safety
To improve image
To improve efficiency
To hire new employees
To improve performance
To increase sales and profits
To help through busy periods
To introduce, facilitate and sustain change
To open up new markets and opportunities
To comply with laws, standards and regulations
To put new systems, methods and practices into use
To confirm their ideas, concepts, plans and strategies
To facilitate transitions, mergers, takeovers and downsizings

---

Fig 1.1

What can consultants do for you?
- ❏ Investigate and objectively assess a problem or an issue
- ❏ Diagnose a problem
- ❏ Recommend a solution
- ❏ Implement or help implement a solution to a particular problem
- ❏ Provide training and teach employees how to solve future problems of a similar nature themselves
- ❏ Manage projects on your behalf
- ❏ Provide updated and accurate information about markets, competitors, new practices and developments
- ❏ Provide professional services – engineering, accounting, recruiting
- ❏ Provide specialist skills as an alternative to employing full-time staff
- ❏ Assist in making business decisions and in business planning
- ❏ Identify alternatives, analyse them and select the most appropriate one.

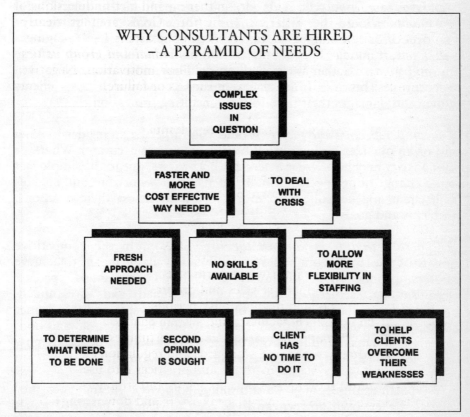

WHY CONSULTANTS ARE HIRED
– A PYRAMID OF NEEDS

COMPLEX ISSUES IN QUESTION

FASTER AND MORE COST EFFECTIVE WAY NEEDED

TO DEAL WITH CRISIS

FRESH APPROACH NEEDED

NO SKILLS AVAILABLE

TO ALLOW MORE FLEXIBILITY IN STAFFING

TO DETERMINE WHAT NEEDS TO BE DONE

SECOND OPINION IS SOUGHT

CLIENT HAS NO TIME TO DO IT

TO HELP CLIENTS OVERCOME THEIR WEAKNESSES

FIG. 1.2

The advantages of using consultants

❑ *Getting a second opinion.* Consultants are generally detached from client organisations and are often used to bring in fresh views and unbiased opinions. In many cases a client investigates a problem or issue, or even actively works on a project, before calling a consultant to help out. This usually happens when some difficulties and obstacles are encountered, but it may also be the case that the client just wants a consultant to confirm the soundness and validity of his views and justify the actions already taken.

❑ *More flexibility in hiring.* Hiring full-time employees is a long, expensive and demanding process. It is also a highly risky one, due to the fact that it may take six months or a year before the unsuitability of a person becomes obvious. With consultants, clients get (or should get) instant expertise and quick results. The engagement is quicker and easier, and termination is just as easy, which is not the case when permanent employees are involved. This doesn't mean that the selection of consultants should be different from the selection of permanent employees. Many clients do a superficial selection job when engaging a consultant, thinking 'They'll only be with us for a relatively short time anyway, so why bother with all those detailed and elaborate selection procedures.' This is a fundamental mistake, one which costs clients money and damages their faith in the consulting profession.

❑ *Fresh perspective and views.* Would you rather be an insider looking out, or an outsider looking in? Which way is more accurate? Whatever your answer may be, there is a need for both views, due to the simple fact that a change of perspective usually opens up new horizons and enables both client and consultant to more accurately assess their positions, problems and goals.

❑ *Expertise that is lacking in the organisation.* In the competitive climate of the 1990s, companies are using all available means to achieve greater productivity, minimise costs and maximise profits. Organisational structures are being redesigned and streamlined, resulting in reduced numbers of core employees and in leaner management structure. All this means that most non-essential and non-core activities, tasks and functions that used to be done in-house are now being contracted out, making it easier to concentrate on the main company business.

A typical example may be a mining company. In the past they generated their own power, ran their own townships, provided meals and accommodation for their workers, had their own engineering departments and employed staff specialists of all kinds. Even in that sort of environment there were many projects of a specialist nature which required consultants' input. Now, most of those activities are contracted out.

The number and scope of consulting and contracting services has swollen dramatically as a result of clients refocusing on their core business. All miscellaneous activities which require expertise that isn't available in-house any more are now being performed under contract. Even companies that employ specialists of various kinds may still lack expertise in certain aspects of those disciplines.

❑ *Opportunity to learn and train employees*. By engaging consultants, clients get a first-class opportunity to observe how consultants do what they do and to adopt their work methods and strategies. Some bold clients even hire consultants to write manuals on the various management methods and strategies which the consultants themselves use, thus effectively eliminating the need for certain consulting services in the future! How's that for a guerrilla tactic?

❑ *The work is performed faster and is of a better quality*. This statement is only true in a general sense. It would be improper and unjust to claim that staff employees are less competent, less profesional and slower producers than outside consultants. However, it is true that consultants generally operate under closer supervision and are normally required to record their activities and hours spent on each activity, which is a less common practice amongst permanent employees. As for the work being of better quality, since consultants are usually specialists in certain fields, in the same allocated time it is likely that they will produce more work of higher quality than non-specialist employees would.

The disadvantages of using consultants

❑ *It is expensive*. Despite the fact that consultants can be engaged at short notice and their assignments terminated the same way, which allows flexibility in hiring and saves associated costs, the fees most consultants charge are simply plain expensive. In most cases, if a client company could hire a suitably qualified and experienced permanent employee who could perform the same tasks as a consultant, it probably would, providing the option saved money. Cost has been, and will be in years to come, the main criterion for either using consultants or employing a full-time person.

❑ *Desired results are not guaranteed*. Many clients, particularly first-time users of consulting services, have a notion that simply by involving a consultant all their problems will be solved. There is nothing further from the truth. Desired results are contingent on many variables: client's and consultant's skills, the quality of their relationship, the organisational climate, timing and appropriateness of actions, cost, time and quality control, and many others. None of these variables guarantees success, but the lack of any of them is likely to cause failure.

❏ *It may create bad vibes amongst employees.* Scenario: an autocratic and ignorant manager doesn't think it's necessary to talk to his employees. When a problem emerges, he calls in consultants, who are welcomed less than enthusiastically and face a climate of bitterness, resentment and suspicion. Employees don't know what consultants are there to do and what effect the project will have on them. They worry about their past mistakes, not realising that consultants are primarily interested in future performance. (The past is important only because it shows weaknesses and trends for the future.) Consultants attempt to involve the workers, but all their efforts hit a brick wall of silence. The project eventually fails, because it isn't the consultant who has to implement the solution, but the employees. The manager fails, because he doesn't realise it isn't management who make or break projects, but the employees. The consultants fail, because they get the blame from the management and diminish their chances of future contracts with the same client. Sound familiar? The biggest fear of the client's employees is not the fear of change, but the fear of the unknown.

❏ *Projects and issues may blow up out of all proportion.* What constitutes an optimum or the best solution to a particular problem is in many cases very difficult to determine. Some theoretical solutions, although they look good on paper, can be extremely difficult, if not impossible, to put into practice. Other solutions, more practical ones, may not be appropriate or feasible enough to warrant implementation.

It is therefore very easy to make the mistake many clients and consultants make – not knowing when and where to stop the consulting process and start implementing the solutions. Compromises have to be made, despite what some perfectionists think. It is in the client's best interests to keep in touch with reality and not to allow consultants to try to iron out every single flaw and imperfection in a system or a solution.

Nice, red, shiny apples

> *Where the broom does not reach, the dust will not vanish of itself.*
> Mao Tse-Tung

The biggest mistake you can make is to believe that, just because they charge a couple of hundred pounds per hour, all consultants are smart and competent. This mistake is common in management circles because it is an easy one to make.

They look smart. Suits, white shirts, latest fashion ties, leather briefcases, executive diaries, creamy, woodfree stationery, mobile telephones, plush offices, private secretaries, mini bars. They talk smart. Profit-loss ratios, empowerment, reengineering, total quality management, positioning, marketing strategies, stock options, yields and bonds, just-in-time manufacturing. They charge smart. Billable hours, reimbursables, travel expenses, research expenses, progress payments.

But some of them are not as smart as they want you to believe. All this masquerade was specifically designed with one aim in mind – to intimidate you! They know that you will judge the quality of their performance on the job by the quality of possessions that surround them. Image manipulation is based on the same premises as the 'beautiful face sells empty mind' tactic. It capitalises on the human tendency to see the surface, not the essence. For some consultants, image is like beauty – skin-deep. Beware of semi-competence, of consultants who appear knowledgeable and professional, but who are much better talkers than doers.

One of the worst disappointments in life is when you bite a nice, red, firm, shiny apple and end up with half a dozen hyperactive worms in your mouth.

Generally, about 10 per cent of consultants are real, outstanding professionals. Another 20 per cent are fully competent and reliable. The rest cover all categories, from acceptable mediocrity to gross incompetence.

Fee-setting

As in any business, fee-setting is crucial for a consultant's success. It is also of vital importance to clients, who pay those fees in return for benefits of equal or, hopefully, greater value. Many consultants price themselves out of the reach of smaller or more price-conscious clients. They are simply perceived as too damn expensive.

Others go to the opposite extreme and set relatively low fees, which only make potential clients suspicious. People associate low prices with lesser quality and unprofessional practices, such as cutting corners or compromising on quality.

Most consulting firms have a set schedule of fees, although they may vary them according to their client's ability to afford those fees. Generally speaking, some educational and non-profit organisations and certain government departments pay lower fees than industrial, mining and manufacturing businesses.

There are many factors that influence both the pricing policies of consulting firms and the fees clients are prepared to pay:

❑ *General condition of the market.* When jobs are scarce, clients dictate the terms and try to squeeze as many concessions as possible out of consultants. A buyers' market makes them choosier and more demanding.

❑ *Firm's reputation and professional standing in business circles.* Reputation is a very powerful bait for clients who don't want surprises, problems or poor quality of service. Fees are dictated by value, and value is based on the firm's standing in the market and the client's perception of that firm.

This is why new consultancies, without reputation or record of success, have trouble finding their first clients. They have to resort to aggressive marketing and sometimes significantly reduced fees to lure clients from existing, established firms. Unless a newcomer positions himself strategically in the market and offers something new, better or different, he'll have a difficult time breaking the ice.

❑ *The nature of the assignment.* Complexity, the client's perception of the difficulty of the tasks involved, and the required level of skill, knowledge and expertise all warrant higher fees. As consultants' roles vary from assignment to assignment, so could their fees vary. Some aggressive firms have no set fees; they vary them to suit each assignment, all aimed at maximising profits.

❑ *Client's perception of expected benefits.* The importance of the project to the client plays a role in setting psychological limits on the fees they are prepared to pay. The higher the perceived value and benefits coming from the results a consultant is expected to achieve, the higher the ceiling on the fees that the client is willing to accept.

❑ *Expenses and desired (or planned) income.* Every consulting firm wants to make profits, so the fee structure is usually arrived at after calculating the break-even figures and then marking them up to establish profit margins. Newcomers to the market are particularly influenced by this arithmetic, because they usually aren't in a position where they can charge the exorbitant fees often quoted by reputable firms.

❑ *Prevailing market rates.* Supply and demand still forms the basis for establishing market rates, in addition to the tradition within a given field. Most clients know what the market rates are and expect consultants to charge around that mark. Significantly higher or lower fees arouse suspicion, and more often than not are the cause of lost assignments.

How do consultants charge for their services?

The two most common ways consultants charge for their services are per hour or per day, and on a retainer basis. Retainers may be for a certain time, say five days every month, or for a specific task that has to be performed. They simply guarantee that the consultant will be available for a certain number of hours per week or per month, should the client need their services. The only problem with retainers is that clients have to pay for the reserved time whether it is used or not.

Fixed-price assignments are what most clients prefer, for obvious reasons. There are no unpleasant surprises: no matter how long it takes to perform the agreed tasks and what difficulties are encountered, it still costs the client the same and the consultant takes all the associated risk.

A special case is a performance- or commission-based fee, where the whole fee or just a portion of it is determined by measuring results and achievements. This may be expressed as amount saved, number of people hired, number of orders received, number of new customers brought in, etc. A fee of this kind is sometimes called a contingency fee, because it is ultimately linked with the project's financial success or failure. This basically means that the consultant gets paid only if he is successful. Not surprisingly most consultants dislike this type of arrangement, while many clients think it is an excellent idea.

Contingency fees

A client complained that he couldn't afford a consultant's hourly fee. 'Instead of doing the job on a time and material basis, I'm willing to do it for a contingency fee,' responded the consultant. 'What is a contingency fee?' asked the client. 'It's very simple. If I don't deliver what I promised, I'll be left with no money at all,' explained the consultant. 'What if you do deliver what you promised?' persisted the client. 'Then *you'll* be left with no money at all,' said the consultant.

How consultants market their services

Advertising methods which work for most other products don't work well in consulting. Promotional campaigns that are often used by other advertisers would only annoy users of consulting services and the whole exercise would be self-defeating. Clients who employ consultants don't get a sudden urge to do so while watching TV or listening to the radio. These media are expensive and not effective for consulting businesses. The printed word is much more productive for most firms. This includes advertising in the Yellow Pages, display advertisements in trade and professional publications, as well as distributing newsletters and leaflets.

Advertising in its standard form is not common in the consulting game. Advanced strategies, however, do work and are used widely. Here are some of them:

❑ *Membership of community organisations and professional institutions.* Becoming well known in a relatively large group of people is a goal for every consultant. They are all potential users of consulting services. Community organisations and professional bodies are a great way to meet people and promote oneself.

❑ *Publishing books and articles.* The easiest way to establish oneself as an expert is to write books or regular articles in professional magazines. Many potential clients will read them and many will contact the author regarding their problems.

❑ *Networking with other consultants.* A very powerful strategy where consultants in non-competitive fields recommend each other to clients when the opportunity presents itself. All firms or individuals working together in this scheme must have the fullest confidence in each other and each other's ability. By making a recommendation, consultants put their credibility on the line, and as we know, credibility is a consultant's most precious possession.

❑ *Speaking at seminars, conferences and other gatherings attended by both clients and consultants.* This sort of exposure is always beneficial. It attracts clients and gives them a golden opportunity to talk to a consultant face-to-face in an informal and intellectually stimulating environment.

❑ *Word-of-mouth advertising – recommendations from satisfied clients.* This is definitely the best advertising a consultant can get. It's reassuring, credible and believable.

Three targets of a client-hunter
1. Clients who already use consulting services of the same or a similar kind.
2. Clients with current needs for consulting services, who are looking to employ a consultant.
3. Clients who are not using consulting services, but would benefit if they did.

How and where do consultants get information about clients? There are many sources:

- ❑ Clients themselves
- ❑ Employees of client's company
- ❑ Annual reports and other client publications (brochures, sales literature, reports)
- ❑ Other consultants who worked for the same client
- ❑ Libraries, magazines, books, press releases
- ❑ Bankers, accountants, business brokers, stock brokers
- ❑ Client's competitors and former employees
- ❑ Suppliers and contractors who had business dealings with the client

A consultant's success depends on two marketing factors: how well he projects the image his clients expect him to project, and how effective he is in convincing prospective clients that he is exactly what those clients are looking for.

In marketing and selling their services, consultants use a dual approach. From the client's perspective, the extrinsic approach emphasises the experience, qualifications and expertise of the consultant. The intrinsic approach places emphasis on the client's needs and the specific benefits consulting services will bring. The aim of the first method is to reduce the client's perception of the risk involved and to convince him that the consultant in question can provide superior services. The aim of the latter method is to convince the client that he needs those services.

Many successful consultants choose and adjust their image to suit clients' expectations. Only when a consultant establishes what the client's needs are can he be sure of what he should offer and what image he should project. The smart approach is to promote the client's image of oneself, rather than one's own. This isn't deceiving, just keeping up appearances and helping clients believe what they want to believe.

The two-stage marketing approach: creating demand
The two-stage marketing approach is the most effective and the most widely used method of attracting clients and expanding a consulting firm's pool of potential users of their services. This is how it works. The consulting firm advertises or sends direct mail invitations for their FREE seminar on a particular topic. The attendees must register (that's how the consulting firm gets their personal and professional details) and the number of seats at the seminar is limited to around twenty to thirty.

After the presentation, which doesn't last long (normally one to three hours), informal discussions take place. A number of attendees, intrigued and hooked by the seminar, will approach the consultants, business cards will be exchanged, problems and fees discussed, and appointments set. Consultants will distribute the firm's capability brochures and try to book as many appointments as possible. This is the first stage. Its main purpose is to identify as many clients as possible.

The second stage focuses on further exploratory meetings with interested clients and on calling the other attendees and trying to go through the same process with them. This demand-creating strategy is quite successful and many consultants use it in some form or other.

The reason why some consultants are in strong demand is that they appear to their clients to be in demand. This is called the law of appearance. Every client wants to deal with consultants who appear successful, because he thinks they are successful. Nobody wants consultants who are desperate to get jobs, who go in begging for business. Clients want what other clients have – consultants in demand.

'Bridging' contracts

Contracts or assignments undertaken by consulting firms to get them through lean periods are called bridging contracts. They are usually won by undercutting competitors' quotes, leaving the desperate consultancy with a small profit, no profit or even a loss. The reasons for quoting ridiculously low fees may vary. The main points are to keep their staff busy, to expand the client base and to gain further expertise in a particular area. Another valid reason could be the intention to win a new client with whom the firm had no previous relationship. This way of entering a new, previously unexploited market is quite common in the cutthroat consulting business.

There are some dangers in using bridging contracts. Firstly, even if the project is carried out to the client's satisfaction, the same client may not like to discover that the fees for future contracts are much higher than the initial, artificially reduced rate. Secondly, if the bridging project continues into a more profitable period for a consultant, future assignments will be at risk due to tied resources, which may even lead to the inability to accept further contracts.

Although the profit motive is of secondary importance in the cases described above, the risk of making an estimating error when quoting for a fixed-price contract is significant. Without the cushioning effect of a healthy profit margin, losses are a very real possiblity.

Smart move
There are quite a few professional organisations for various types of consultants. Find out when and where their next meeting, conference or seminar is going to be held and attend it. It will be an invaluable educational lesson.

The intangible aspects of a consulting firm

A *witchdoctor image*
To many business people, consultants and their profession are still surrounded by mystique and lack of real comprehension of what they do and how they operate. Where consultants are concerned, many managers are in *terra incognita*, with very few landmarks to guide them.

This lack of clear understanding is made worse by some members of the consultancy profession, who, if not deliberately, then through a silent code of practice, try to disguise and obscure their methods and means. Many professional individuals and managers, especially ones in smaller companies with restricted budgets, have never had a chance to hire a consultant and learn about their ways of doing business. When they come into contact with consultants and contractors for the first time, they lack a thorough understanding of the client-consultant relationship, as well as of the likely benefits and possible pitfalls of that arrangement.

Being an electrical engineer by education, I can confirm a sad fact about most engineering courses. Not only were we not taught about the maintenance aspect of engineering, project and contract management, financial control and management of resources (including consultants, technicians, draftsmen and contractors), those things weren't even mentioned in our curriculum. It was as though its creators assumed that we would all go quietly about our business, ignore reality and work diligently all our lives in a research lab or design firm, with our noses close to the grindstone, without any contact with such 'trivialities', which are less important than 'pure engineering science' anyway.

As always happens in life, people who don't learn in school learn from experience; theirs and that of others. But experience is the worst teacher – it sets the test before giving the lesson. It is also an expensive way to learn, and somebody has to pay for it. Employers are less prepared than ever to finance their employees' education – they want fast results, quick fixes and a healthy bottom line.

The consulting services market resembles a diamond shop. There are some big stones, some small ones and some tiny ones, in all possible colours and cuts. They all sparkle and produce brilliant, shiny effects, and they all carry a similar price tag. But only some of them are genuine gems; the rest are cubic zirconia, without any real value whatsoever. The problem is, in that shop there are no certificates. You, the client, have to develop an eye for the real gems and distinguish between the 'sinks' and the 'floats'.

Salesmanship

For some consultants, the worst offence is to call them 'salesmen'. Although selling is the core activity in the consulting profession, the one that underlies all other dimensions of the profession profile, it is almost always looked down upon.

No matter what consultants themselves may feel, like or dislike, the fact is that experience, knowledge and expertise, which are all required in order to do a quality job for a client, are far from enough to win a contract. The firm has to sell itself to a client, to create the right impressions and be viewed as the best match for a problem a client may have.

No matter how creative, innovative, efficient or progressive a consulting firm may be, it won't get very far if it isn't able to sell all these qualities. Clients who can recognise those traits that can lead to potential benefits for them are rare. Most have to be convinced through hard sell and persuasion.

Indeed, most consultants do sell very well. They look good, they project self-confidence and generate an atmosphere of enthusiasm and achievement. They simply have to. Selling intangible and expensive consulting services to a tough and sophisticated market saturated with competition is not a job for the faint-hearted.

When selling their services to prospective clients, consultants deal with clients' needs. There are two types of needs – the felt needs and the created needs. Felt needs are those that originate with the clients, the ones clients feel without being persuaded, prompted or influenced by anybody else, including the consultants. The created needs are a result of persuasion or inducement by consultants, who sell an idea by emphasising benefits and making clients feel a need for consulting services which they didn't feel before.

The 80/20 rule of competence

Eighty per cent of problems solved by consultants are 'common sense' problems. The other 20 per cent are challenging assignments, in which they have to show what they are made of.

What makes consultants effective is how well they apply their expertise to a particular customer's problem and how well they plan, manage, integrate and implement solutions. Solutions always bring changes. Those changes have to be accepted, implemented and assimilated by client companies, but most importantly, they have to produce measurable results which will help clients to gain an advantage over their competitors.

Managers usually think that consultants are walking encyclopedias. This stereotype is very far from reality. No one knows everything, and consultants are no exception. What consultants do know, however, is where to get the information their clients need. All they have to do is find it, or, as happens in real life, get a clerk, an assistant or an apprentice to find it for them. It goes without saying that the clients still get charged the full fee although the actual work is performed by juniors.

Competence is an unequivocal prerequisite for any professional's success, although a very hard one to define. How to distinguish an expert from a just competent consultant, or from a complete dud? Clients usually define competence as the way in which individual and collective attributes and resources, such as skills, knowledge, experience, time and attitudes, are called upon and utilised in projects and assignments.

It simply isn't enough to focus on a consultant's individual qualities, such as educational qualifications, membership of professional bodies and previous experience. Since most consulting work is done in a complex and changing environment, there are a number of external factors that may have an impact on the standard of the work and on the failure or success of projects. These outside factors require certain qualities, such as good communication skills, adaptability, a highly organised personality and the understanding of broader concepts and values.

Credibility, reputation and professionalism

> A friend: 'You were once unemployed yourself. How can you justify taking people's jobs away?'
> Outplacement consultant: 'It keeps me employed.'

Definition: credibility gap – the difference between what one says and what one does.

Remember that word: credibility? You won't hear it too often these days, I guarantee. How does that sound? 'I guarantee'? Does that make

---

Smart move
Always do what you promised you would do. Close that credibility gap. In other words, practise what you preach. Of course, demand the same from the consultants you employ.

me credible? Or 'Trust me, I know what I'm doing!' Do you feel convinced? Of course not, one doesn't gain credibility through empty slogans and clichés. Credibility is gained by keeping promises and appointments and by practising what one preaches. People become credible if they live by their philosophy and put their words into action.

In a service-providing business generally, and especially in a knowledge-orientated business such as consulting, credibility and reputation are crucial for survival in the tough cut-throat arena in which consulting companies compete.

To a very large extent, the credibility and professional image of a company determine how much business that consultancy will obtain. Reputation precedes both clients and consultants, but it's always the clients who use it as a crucial criterion in evaluating proposals, tenders and applications and in awarding contracts.

Establishing credibility and reputation is a slow and painstaking process, but losing them can happen overnight, and that is the worst fear of every consulting firm.

Insensitive comments and remarks, lack of appreciation of a client's point of view, being late in submitting a report or a proposal, poor quality of work and reports, a project that runs late or over budget, tasks that have to be redone, are all dark stains on the white collar of a consultant.

Confidentiality and trust

> *You can learn good manners to deal with people, but you can't learn*
> *to trust people. And you must trust to be comfortable with them.*
> Peter Drucker

There is a magic word that opens many doors. That word is *trust*. Apart from the matter of the competency and professionalism of the consultants you employ, confidentiality and trust should be your main concerns as a client. Consultants, because of the nature of their involvement with clients, have insight into the very core of clients' organisations. They have access to confidential documents, reports, studies, drawings, forecasts, business plans. They know how various departments operate, how they relate to each other, who the managers are and what their strengths and weaknesses are.

One way of protecting your company's confidentiality and trade secrets is to develop an intellectual property and confidentiality agreement, which will stipulate that everything a consulting company creates in the course of its assignment becomes the property of the client. It should also specify that a consultant will not divulge any internal information about a client to other clients. Should this matter go before a court, a client will usually have to prove that the information disclosed was in fact a trade secret that could be used to its owner's detriment.

One could always argue that there is no way of preventing consultants from using the knowledge gained during previous assignments later on, while doing jobs of a similar nature. Most clients normally accept this as a fact of life and prefer to rely on consultants' discretion and professionalism. Intellectual property agreements and confidentiality agreements are rarely worth the paper they are printed on. Trust is always the most effective way of dealing with the complexities of client-consultant relationships.

How consultants establish trust

> *Alice could not help her lips curling up into a smile as she began: 'Do you know, I always thought Unicorns were fabulous monsters, too! I never saw one alive before!'*
> *'Well, now that we have seen each other,' said the Unicorn, 'if you'll believe in me, I'll believe in you. Is that a bargain?'*
> *'Yes, if you like' said Alice.*
> Lewis Carroll, *Through the Looking-Glass*

- ❑ By being friendly and polite
- ❑ By establishing common ground with clients
- ❑ By giving honest, candid opnions
- ❑ By being businesslike and professional
- ❑ By displaying empathy and understanding of client's problems
- ❑ By talking benefits and solutions
- ❑ By being action-orientated
- ❑ By emphasising quality
- ❑ By demonstrating professionalism and competence
- ❑ By accepting responsibility for the outcome of their actions
- ❑ By showing determination to get the job done and dedication to the project
- ❑ By discussing the pros and cons of every action, option and solution

Through my experience in dealings with consultants I discovered an interesting truth: the most believable consultants are those who admit their flaws, inadequacies and mistakes. Showing a human side always goes a long way towards winning a client's trust. Nobody knows everything, but this is a difficult admission to make for most consultants. Those who do admit that they don't know an answer to a particular question or that they haven't had the particular experience the client is after are generally more successful in winning assignments than those who claim they know everything.

Imagine yourself in a car dealer's yard, buying a second-hand car. How do you feel if a salesperson generally compliments you on your choice, but also points out a couple of imperfections and slight problems with the particular vehicle you have chosen? Would that win your confidence? You bet it would! And those are the same tactics a shrewd consultant uses to win a client's trust.

Ethics

> The louder he talked of his honour, the faster we counted our spoons.
>
> Ralph Waldo Emerson

There is no fixed code of ethics that guides the consulting profession. Since consultants need no licence to operate nor a membership in a recognised body that would set rules and enforce regulations for them to comply to, each firm or individual performs under their own moral and ethical standards.

Moral and ethical values cannot be enforced or proclaimed in a consulting company's mission statement. They have to be written in the hearts of individuals and they have to come from there. Universities and business schools concentrate on techniques and ignore issues such as ethics, values and moral standards.

Although some experts claim that ethics can be taught, an individual's ethical standing is usually determined by his family background, personality and past experience. The same applies to consulting firms. They are only as ethical as the individuals who work for them. The bottom line in every organisation is the individual. A company cannot change the individual's views, which are more or less already formed, but the individual can change a company, which is constantly shifting as a consequence of interaction and synergy between employees.

The games consultants play

> 'I've received information that the majority of staff you employ often have little or no consulting experience and that they usually receive salaries of between six and eight thousand pounds a year. That's under two hundred pounds a week. Yet you charge two thousand pounds a week for their services. Even allowing for hotel and travel costs,' the politician grinned, 'that's a fairly healthy profit margin,

wouldn't you say?'

'Mr Pringle,' Marker made little attempt to hide his scorn, 'in our business we have no time for people who have no urge to excel. Yes, we do have a large number of less experienced staff on a modest salary. But that is only so that the ambitious will be encouraged to fight for promotion and the mediocre forced to leave. That is why we are successful, we invest in the strong, we get rid of the weak.' Marker's eyes blazed. 'If some other people ran their companies that way, then maybe they'd be a lot damn healthier than they are.'

Neil Martin, *The American Way*

Quoting low, billing high

> *The house of delusion is cheap to build but draughty to live in.*
> A. E. Housman

Consulting is generally a boom and bust business. Getting a steady inflow of work has always been one of the most desired aims for consultants. When business is quiet, many firms opt for a minimalistic approach. They charge just enough not to lose money, just enough to keep their people employed. When it comes to tendering, this usally means undercutting other consultants' quotes (see 'Bridging' contracts, p.22).

Clients are almost always tempted by low quotes, which is understandable if human nature is taken into account. This may be called 'maximising one's returns'. Everybody wants as much as possible while giving away as little as possible.

There are, however, two intrinsic dangers where low quotes are concerned. Firstly, to minimise costs, consultants will have to take many short cuts, the overall quality of the work will suffer and the client will end up with a 'prematurely born baby', which will require months and months of nursing (i.e., the job will have to be redone).

The second danger is even more common. During the course of the assignment, more and more obstacles, unpredictable difficulties and additional expenses will be encountered, and the client will end up with an additional bill, in some cases even higher than the original quote. This effectively means that the job will cost twice as much, which will naturally leave the client infuriated. Experienced bidders can determine if there is a chance of changes in the work later, after the contract is awarded, so they bid a break-even or below-cost price, knowing they can recover their profits by charging for the additional costs and negotiating the changes later. This offer of the smallest quantities, specifications and hours that appear credible in a proposal is called a 'low ball'.

Use of junior staff

We have already seen that consultants who 'sell' a consulting firm and negotiate the deal don't necessarily do the work. The majority of tasks are performed by much less experienced and knowledgeable junior consultants. Although this practice is generally sound and ethical, there is one fundamental danger associated with it: if less experienced performers are being used, the work may take longer than anticipated in the consultant's proposal. In the case of fixed-price contracts, the consulting firm will have to bear the consequences. If the contract is on time and material (reimbursable basis), the client will have to pay for the consultant's inefficiency and inexperience.

Can do, been there, done that (dangers of standard solutions)

Consultants are, or at least should be, systematic thinkers and problem-solvers. Through their assignments they develop a structured way of thinking and analysing problems. These experiences lead them to sets of patterned approaches. Through these approaches they sort, group, systematise and interrelate concepts, problems and issues.

Although this type of organised thinking is usually beneficial to both parties, it carries within itself a major potential danger – the danger of labelling and classifying situations into neat boxes and viewing them as they should be instead of as they really are. Once issues are labelled and classified, the second mistake is to apply pre-engineered methods and search for general solutions, instead of tailoring them to the unique circumstances of each particular assignment.

Generalising is a dangerous practice, although widely used by consultants when competing for jobs. It's incredible how every firm claims they can do everything (or almost everything), even individual freelancers. Whatever the issue is, they've been there and done that (or at least something similar). Beware of these Jacks of all trades!

Reinventing the wheel (dangers of non-standard solutions)

There are two fundamental approaches to consulting. Traditional consulting firms look at every assignment from a different perspective. They assume that every problem is unique and different from others, and therefore requires a new solution. Non-traditional or unconventional firms use consulting methods based on standard, universal solutions. They claim that clients' problems are not unique. No matter what discipline they involve – management, engineering, marketing, finances – they are just more or less similar replicas of problems faced by other clients.

The consultants of the first kind quite often reinvent the wheel, and clients ultimately end up paying more than in the case of adaptation and customisation of standard solutions.

Keep the price, change the package

This is one of the shrewdest tactics consultants use. It applies to situations where clients either cannot afford certain services and ask for a lower price, or can afford the price but want more in return for their money.

Simply stated, in the first case, the consultant will quote the lower price, which is within the client's reach, but will also scale down their services. In the second case, they will include the additional tasks the client wants them to do, but will also increase the total price for the package. The tactic can be summed up as: 'For this price we'll give you this package, for a different price there is a different package.'

As you can see, it's a very convenient method for avoiding making concessions when pressured by a tough client's negotiators.

Charging for what they know and do, instead of for what they produce

You have probably heard Avis's famous slogan, 'We are number two. We try harder.' But did you know that Avis is still number two among car rental companies? Obviously, trying harder isn't enough. Yet this is exactly what most clients do and where many of them fail. They don't realise that consultants should be paid on the basis of what they produce, not on the basis of the motions they go through or the unapplied knowledge they may have. The efforts they put in are not the ultimate aim. They are just the means of getting there.

Clients don't pay consultants on the basis of what they know or are able to do. The important thing is that clients want people who take action, use their knowledge and skills to solve problems and, ultimately, create profits for them. Remember, buy results, not efforts. Trying is one thing, achieving is something completely different.

Advocating teamwork

A mediocre consulting company is as good as the individuals working for it. A top consulting firm is better than the sum of its individuals' skills and knowledge. This synergetic aspect of the consulting business has constantly been perpetuated through business articles and books, usually written by consultants themselves. Although this fact generally stands the scrutiny, the truth is slightly different. Consulting firms don't carry out assignments. Individuals do.

The success or failure of a consulting project ultimately rests on the narrow shoulders of an individual. Pretending that the success of an assignment is the achievement of a firm is a plot of the mediocre majority in those firms. As in any business setting, there are some outstanding consultants, many mediocre ones and the odd incompentent. Usually, financial rewards are not directly proportional to an individual's achievements and performance. The top individuals are undercompensated and the incompetent ones are overcompensated.

By selling teamwork instead of individuals, consulting firms increase their chances of selling the underachievers together with the overachievers. Individual, self-employed consultants depend on their own skills and nothing else. This is not the case with the individuals employed by larger consultancies.

Making promises they cannot keep

> Take some more tea,' the March Hare said to Alice, very earnestly.
> 'I've had nothing yet,' Alice replied in an offended tone, 'so I can't take more.'
> 'You mean you can't take less,' said the Hatter. 'It's very easy to take more than nothing.'
> 'Nobody asked your opinion,' said Alice.
> Lewis Carroll, *Alice's Adventures in Wonderland.*

In the frenzy and excitement every consultant feels when faced with the prospect of winning an assignment, making a rushed, snappy statement, promise or commitment is very easy. When the excitement passes, those promises and commitments are usually forgotten or overlooked by the consultant. The client, however, never forgets or overlooks them.

Even if the project turns out to be a success, clients may feel disappointed and bitter. Every consultant knows that not keeping promises is the surest way to losing clients. Some backyard operators, however, would do (and promise) anything just to get their foot in the door. Make sure they stay where they belong – outside.

When faced with an assignment beyond their capabilities or expertise, a consultant has three basic options. The first is to decline the assignment. The second is to accept the assignment and subcontract certain parts of the job to other consulting specialists, while retaining overall responsibility for the project. The third option is to advise the client on the issue and ask them to employ another specialist for those tasks the consultant knows he can't carry out to the client's satisfaction.

Using the boundaries strategy

Children use the 'boundaries' tactic all the time. It's their favourite game. When they do something for the first time, they carefully observe their parents to see what their reaction will be. If there is no feedback, children assume that what they have just done is acceptable and will be tolerated in the future. It will act as a milestone that will mark the boundaries of their behaviour.

At work, some consultants also use this tactic. They try to establish what is the minimum or maximum they can get away with in each situation. That will indicate the limits within which they'll have to operate.

Almost everybody intuitively knows the minimum they have to achieve in order to stay employed. In every organisation, there are unwritten quotas to be met and criteria of performance to be satisfied. The sooner consultants find out what they are, the easier it is for them to set the pace and establish themselves in a new environment.

Riding on a subcontractor's back

This involves the use of another consulting company, with a solid reputation and expertise, as a subcontractor to the consulting company which is bidding for the job. By including the name of a reputable company in their proposal, a troubled consultancy with a tarnished image and shaky reputation tries to lure a client into giving them a job. Of course, the 'bait' consultant will do only a minor portion of the work, the majority of which will be performed by the bidding consultant.

Erecting fences (excuses, excuses . . .)

When a consultant is about to start diagnosing a problem and says something like 'The short-sightedness of past management and the lack of progressive monitoring and controlling methods has resulted in a culture unsupportive to change and implementation of new methods and recommendations' he is merely leaving his escape hatch open and looking for someone else to blame for something he hasn't even done yet. This is a typical example of fence-erecting.

Fences can be erected anywhere, at any time. All that is needed is suitable soil and a hammer to drive the pickets in. Suitable soil is abundant in any organisation. It comes in various forms:

❑ Mistakes of past and current management
❑ Errors, omissions and shoddy work of previous consultants and contractors
❑ Unsupportive corporate climate
❑ Lack of client resources and funding

Clients' fears about consultants

> *Life is too short to live with a bad deal.*
> David Geffen, talent agent and recording executive

People are creatures of habit and fears. Clients especially so. One of the main reasons why many clients resent dealing with consultants is that they fear the whole concept of consulting. The consulting business is intangible, fickle and risky. When clients buy goods and some services, they know exactly what to expect and can relate to the finished product or performed job from the beginning. It is seldom so with consulting.

Clients' fears are numerous and ever-present:

❏ *The fear of the unknown.* Many potential users of consulting services, in real need of outside help, even after long deliberation don't seem to be able to make a decision to hire a consultant. Their fear is a very common one – the fear of the unknown.

The questions that rush through their minds are numerous: How do consultants work? How do they charge? Am I going to be charged for the initial consultation? Can I afford their services? What can I expect in return for my money? What will my commitments be? How and when would I be able to break the contract? What will the legal implications be?

❏ *Once bitten, twice shy.* Some managers who have had dealings with consultants before, may have had bad experiences. Perhaps they were overcharged or the consultant underdelivered. Maybe the whole project turned out to be a real fiasco and the manager's reputation and chances for promotion were damaged.

These managers will be guarded and reserved. Although they may need consultants' skills, they will be fearful and suspicious.

❏ *The matter of trust.* Some clients feel uncomfortable with the fact that after paying substantial consulting fees, they won't have any guarantee that they will get value for money. These are usually the managers who tend to 'play it safe'. They forget that business life is generally unsafe, unpredictable and uncertain. Some trust is expected as a bond between a client and a consultant.

❏ *The matter of competence.* This fear is linked to the previous one; they share the common denominator, of value for money. Here, the client subconsciously questions the consultant's competence. Have they got enough knowledge and experience to handle the project? Can they produce results efficiently? Am I going to end up paying for their education and sponsor their learning exercise?

> **Empty desk syndrome**
> A new client, visiting a consultant's office, noticed the neat appearance of his desk.
> 'You know the old saying,' said the consultant, 'a cluttered desk reflects a cluttered mind.'
> 'I agree with that,' replied the client. 'What worries me is the fact that your desk is empty.'

❏ *Fear of failure.* Fear of failure is a powerful fear. It makes people less willing to experiment, to explore or to try new ways, methods or consulting firms.

❏ *Fear of change.* Consultants are change merchants: one way or another they always bring change to their clients. Every change brings the unknown, and the unknown always produces fear, which clients associate with consultants. This vicious circle is not easy to break. One of the best ways to do it is to learn about consultants, know how they operate and make eliminating fear of change your main goal. This book should help you do that.

The acceptance and success of any change depends heavily on the quality of the relationship between the change agent (the consultant) and the organisation that is to be changed. The deeper the change and the greater the uneasiness it produces, the more effective and close a relationship is needed.

What to do about your fears

You may be an experienced user of consulting services or a first-timer who is thinking about hiring a consultant. No matter which group you belong to, you'll have your fears, doubts and dilemmas. This is perfectly normal in any relationship, and the best way to deal with it is to face your fears. Don't try to close your eyes and hope they'll disappear. They won't. Face them one by one and analyse them soberly and rationally. Ask yourself some funamental questions:

❏ Where are these fears coming from?
❏ What or who is causing them?
❏ How are others dealing with their fears?
❏ What are my ideas on overcoming these fears?

Also talk to some consultants. Don't be afraid of appearing uninformed and overcautious. Nobody knows everything and everybody lives with fears and uneasiness. Consultants will understand. Anyway, if you knew everything, you wouldn't need them, would you? It is in their best interests to help you overcome your fears, so you can be sure they'll go a long way to accommodate you by answering your questions and addressing your concerns.

Chapter 2: Selecting Consultants

Hire the right consultant for the right job

How good are MBAs really?

> *I am not impressed by diplomas. They don't do the work. My marks were not as good as those of others, and I didn't take the final examination. The principal called me in and said I have to leave. I told him that I didn't want a diploma. They had less value than a cinema ticket. A ticket at least guaranteed that you would get in. A diploma guaranteed nothing.*
>
> Soichiro Honda

Your goal, as a manager who deals with consultants on a regular basis, is to deploy people with 'real-life' experience and practical skills, not theorists hiding behind their MBA credentials.

An MBA is not a standardised product and many programmes don't offer much value. An MBA degree is not a substitute for on-the-job experience. The best it can do is provide a frame of reference and knowledge of general principles of management, so when a consultant is faced with a problem he's never encountered before, he'll know how to go about it, how the pieces of a puzzle fit together and where to start looking for solutions.

The emphasis in business schools' curricula is still primarily on the analytical, quantitative, logical and systematic aspects and methods of management. That is what professors teach and are able to evaluate and that is what the Western management system values as central and fundamental for success.

However, the signs of change are evident in some courses. After years of criticism from employers that schools are turning out narrow-viewed, numbers-minded analysts, business schools are adding more courses in 'soft' skills, such as teamwork, leadership and motivation. There is also more emphasis on quality, customer satisfaction and on teaching students to see the big picture – business as a whole, instead of as a collection of disparate functions.

Is your company an educational institution for greenhorn consultants?

'I'm afraid you've not had much practice in riding,' she ventured to say, as she was helping him up from his fifth tumble.
The Knight looked very much surprised, and a little offended at the remark. 'What makes you say that?' he asked, as he scrambled back into the saddle, keeping hold of Alice's hair with one hand, to save himself from falling over on the other side.
'Because people don't fall off quite so often, when they've had much practice.'
'I've had plenty of practice,' the Knight said very gravely: 'plenty of practice.'

Lewis Carroll, *Through the Looking-Glass*

The biggest mistake consultants can make is to imply that they have never made a mistake. Never hire those with that sort of claim. Why is that so?

Firstly, it is very likely they are not telling the truth. Everybody makes mistakes. Even if it's true, stay away from them. You should hire people who have had their wins and losses. That experience gives those consultants the strength and knowledge of how to capitalise on their losses and the ability to do a better job the next time by not repeating the same mistakes.

People who never make mistakes and haven't had to overcome barriers will fall on their face when they hit the first obstacle. Clients don't like to pay for consultants' mistakes and are not prepared to finance their 'education'. They prefer people whose former clients paid for the mistakes made.

Smart Move
Look for people who are fun to work with. They smile, play and enjoy themselves while producing results. They also make everyone around them feel better. They are the spreaders of enthusiasm germs. Beware: enthusiasm is highly contagious!

A profile of a competent consultant

I am sure that, at this point, if you could, you would ask me one simple question: How do I know which consultants to engage and which to stay away from? The honest answer would be that the selection rules aren't clear-cut and aren't a sufficient protection from being taken advantage of later on. If the opposite was true, the best consultants would get all assignments and the rest would be knocked out.

Since we know that's not the case, either the rules are not definite or employers don't make enough effort or exercise enough caution when selecting consultants. It is possible that there are elements of both.

The checklist that follows asks some questions that could help you concentrate on finding the right answers about a consultant's background:

❑ *Qualifications.* Has the consultant the formal qualifications to do the job? Does he know how to do the job? Are his qualifications recognised in the industry as appropriate for this particular kind of project?

❑ *Experience.* How relevant is the consultant's experience? How much experience does he have and how could you benefit from that experience?

❑ *Motivation.* How motivated is the consultant? What motivates him – money, sense of achievement, praise, working conditions, a promise of future contracts if succssful? Is he a self-starter or does he need some supervision?

❑ *Communication skills.* Can the candidate express himself in writing and in good grammatical form? Can he express himself orally in individual and group situations? Is he a good listener? Can he effectively communicate his ideas and explain and present solutions and proposals?

❑ *Maturity and emotional stability.* Is he able to cope with stress and pressures that are likely to be encountered during the project? Is he a mature and responsible person who can make decisions and assume responsibility? Is he emotionally stable and fair and consistent in his dealings with his peers and clients?

Your first job

A consultant answered an ad to work with a businessman. At the interview the proprietor said that his business wasn't going well. He was losing money. He was worried about it but he didn't have time to both worry and do the work that was necessary to save the business.

He wanted to devote himself to his business and pay the consultant to do all the worrying – about quality control, about payments due, about profit and loss ratios, about anything at all that needed worrying about.

He was willing to pay handsomely for the consultant's time. They settled on an annual fee of $67,000 plus a liberal expense allowance.

The consultant agreed, but said, 'If you're in such trouble, where are you going to get the $67,000 to pay me?'

The man said, 'That's your first worry.'

G. and L. Perret, *Gene Perret's Funny Business*

Things to look for in a consultant

❑ Professional qualifications and relevant experience in the required discipline.
❑ The capacity to communicate important ideas and concepts in a clear and effective way.
❑ A reference list of satisfied clients.
❑ A thorough understanding of the client's business and the industry the client is in.
❑ The ability to find and implement innovative and effective solutions to challenging problems.
❑ A genuine interest in the client's organisation, dedication to its goals and objectives and commitment to helping achieve them.

Evaluation and selection

Basic selection criteria

> *The price of ability does not depend on merit, but on supply and demand.*
> George Bernard Shaw, 'Socialism and Superior Brains' in *Fortnightly Review*, April 1894

There are three basic criteria for selecting consultants:

1. They can and will do a good job for you
2. They will make you look good in your boss's eyes
3. They will justify your decision to hire them by their performance and achievements on the assignment

Selecting a consultant who is best suited for the assignment is far from trivial. To the inexperienced eye and less probing mind of a typical client, the difference between the fundamental characteristics of competing consulting firms is not at all significant. Therefore, when a choice has to be made, it is usually based on variations of marginal importance, such as the impact of consultants' presentations, the quality of proposals or the personal feelings of the client. Clients are no different from the average consumers of other, more prosaic goods. Their choice isn't always conscious, deliberate or fully backed up by reason.

The selection interview question sheet

Specific questions about your project:
- ❏ How confident are you in your ability to handle this project?
- ❏ Should you be successful in getting this contract, when could you start?
- ❏ Tell me about some of the first things you would do on this project.
- ❏ What documents and records would you need?
- ❏ How long do you envisage the whole job would take?
- ❏ How many people would be assigned to the job? What would their roles be?
- ❏ Who will manage the project?
- ❏ Would your involvement be intermittent or continuous until completion?
- ❏ What help would you need from us?
- ❏ Would there be any potential disruptions of our normal operations?
- ❏ What information methods would you use?
- ❏ What general approach to this assignment would you use?
- ❏ How do you see this assignment? Where do you think problems could come from?
- ❏ _____
- ❏ _____
- ❏ _____
- ❏ _____

Interviewing consultants

No matter how thoroughly you've analysed a consultant's proposals and quotes, investigated the firm's background and experience, and checked references with former clients, you would be making a cardinal mistake if you didn't meet the consultant in person. Even telephone contacts won't suffice. Only in a face-to-face meeting will you be able to evaluate him fully and make a wise and prudent decision about engaging him or giving a chance to someone else.

Consultants who can talk well about themselves, their experience, education and past achievements, who can project (I didn't say possess) integrity, sincerity and a real interest in clients, are the ones who get assignments. The others, often more experienced, intelligent and hard-working individuals and firms, who are not as good at marketing their services and selling themselves to prospective clients, more often than not don't get what they deserve – the plum jobs! What an irony!

Asking the right questions at the right time is the essence of success in every selection process. To properly evaluate various aspects of a consultant's background, knowledge, experience, expertise, personality and capability, a structured questioning plan will prove a productive and infallible tool in every client's hand. A properly devised questioning strategy can reveal a lot. It gives an interviewer a clear idea about which questions should be asked, in what order, how and why. Don't be satisfied with vague, theoretical or future-oriented answers. Ask for specific, experience-related examples from the consultant's past. Each case should address all three basic aspects of any behavioural situation:

1. The *situation* (problem) that existed or *task* that had to be performed
2. The specific *action* taken or not taken by a consultant (and why or why not)
3. The *results* or consequences of the *action* (or the lack of it)

The image test
One of the most revealing questions you may ask during the evaluation interview is 'Tell us in a minute or two why should we hire you in preference to other consultants.' The answers to this question are always illustrative.

People and reputation

The two things you should be most concerned about when selecting a consulting firm of any speciality and in any business don't appear in its proposals, capability statements, shareholders' reports or monthly newsletters. They have to be found out. They are its people and its reputation.

Enthusiasm and challenge

> There are one-storey intellects, two-storey intellects, and three-storey intellects with skylights. All fact-collectors, who have no aim beyond their facts, are one-storey men. Two-storey men compare, reason, generalise, using the labours of fact-collectors as well as their own. Three-storey men idealise, imagine, predict; their best illumination comes from above, through the skylight.
>
> Oliver Wendell Holmes

One man's boring job is someone else's challenge. The same applies to consultants. Enthusiasm is a quality relatively hard to find. When you do find it, appreciate it. Hire it. Enthusiasm is worth paying for, because enthusiasm produces results and gets the job done. Apathy, routine and complacency don't.

Visionaries and hired guns
Three consultants are working on a similar job: devising a marketing strategy for a client. When asked about what their job was, these were the answers: 'Working on advertisements,' said the first consultant. 'Earning a living,' said another. 'Helping to build a first-class company,' replied the third one. Which one would you hire?

The right cultural and personal fit

In the past, consultants were hired for their ability to talk. Now they get selected for their ability to listen.

Companies think in various ways, they value different things and use different styles – leadership styles, problem-solving styles, communicating styles, project management styles, decision-making styles. A good match between a client organisation and a consulting team (or individual) is critically important for success.

Culture is a mixture of values, beliefs, rules, stereotypes, rituals and taboos. Culture defines the company's philosophy, the way it handles business, the way it treats its employees (including consultants) and the way it responds to change.

The basis for a successful client-consultant relationship is the consultant's understanding of the industry and the market that a particular client operates in, as well as his understanding and knowledge of the client's business and corporate policies and objectives. Such understanding is necessary to ensure that consulting services are delivered in a way that is consistent with, not in contradiction to (as happens in many cases), the client's values, practices and overall corporate philosophy.

The rapport between a client and a consultant may determine the outcome of the whole relationship. Clients would rather deal with consultants they like, trust and feel comfortable with than with those they don't know, don't like or have doubts about. The price may be right, the proposal may be a masterpiece of modern literature and an example of consulting craft and mastery, but if the chemistry between the two is not right, the whole relationship will end before it actually began and no contract will be signed. However, it is important not to confuse likeability with capability. Understand that the best-qualified consultant is not necessarily the one you like or the one you are friends with.

Experience

> *Experience is the name everyone gives to his mistakes.*
> Oscar Wilde, *Lady Windermere's Fan*

There are three basic concerns for clients:

1. *Can the consultant do the job?* This question evaluates the consultant's expertise, knowledge and experience. Are they capable of performing the task you want them to perform? Have they done it before? How well did they do it and how successful was the outcome of their past effort?

2. *Will the consultant do the job?* This question raises the issue of intent and goal. What is the consultant's aim? Are they committed to finding solutions to problems and producing results for you, or just making their best effort and going through the motions? Are they after a contract simply to keep themselves busy over the quiet period or are they really dedicated to your cause?

3. *Will the consultant fit into the organisation?* This is a question of compatibility between consultant and client. How experienced are they in working with people from various backgrounds and with different attitudes and work methods? Will they be able to operate at an optimum level, or will their performance be hindered by the client's environment – policies, restrictions, inefficiencies, fears, habits, culture?

The problem with evaluating capability and experience is that consultants judge themselves by what they feel capable of doing, while clients judge them by what they have already done.

Reference-checking

> *It is hard to believe that a man is telling the truth when you know that you would lie if you were in his place.*
> H. L. Mencken

Telephone reference checks are very revealing. When you talk to the consultant's previous clients, look for a reluctance or hesitancy on the referee's part. It is much more difficult to praise people in person than in writing.

The name of the referee will always be given to you by the consultant. By choosing loyal referees consultants try to increase their chances of passing the reference checks. This is all very well, by all means talk to nominated clients. If you know of any other clients the consultant in question has worked for, you should get in touch with them, too. By using this strategy you can get a 'second opinion', which is usually more realistic and less favourable, due to the fact that a second referee wasn't selected by the consultants themselves.

When you speak to the previous clients of a consultant you want to employ, use some of the 'hard' questions listed below.

Some reference-checking questions:
- ❏ Would you engage them again without hesitation?
- ❏ The assignment we are recruiting for is very challenging. It needs a consultant with strong specialist skills. Do you really think they have what it takes?
- ❏ What did they achieve while working for you? Did they meet the criteria required for the job?
- ❏ What plans did you have for the consultant? Have you used them again since?
- ❏ How do they compare with other firms in this field?
- ❏ Did you feel comfortable working with them? How did they fit into your company?
- ❏ Did they finish the project on time and within budget? What methods, techniques and solutions were used?
- ❏ Where would you say their strengths and weaknesses lie?
- ❏ Are there any other particular issues that we should be aware of?

Self-terminating quality

The best consultants make sure that once a job is done, you no longer need them. They see to it that you become familiar with the solution and have confidence in it. They hand over the ownership of the solution to you and empower you to be self-sufficient. Mediocre consultants intentionally or unintentionally never implement the solutions fully and there are always omissions and final details to be ironed out, which means that they have to come back again and again.

Bad consultants make sure you remain dependent on them for ever, making you a steady source of revenue. They don't involve you in details, don't train you properly in solutions and systems they've implemented or installed, and never completely finish the job, so there's always something missing or 'not quite right'.

> **Mental exercise**
> How do you make a decision when selecting consultants? Why do
> you select those you do and reject the others? Is it because they are
> the only ones you know of? Or because they quote the lowest price?
> Or because they are famous and reputable? Because they are
> friendly and supportive? What edge have they got over the others?
> How did they position themselves to gain that edge? Analyse your
> selection methods and identify your criteria. Are you happy with
> them? Is improvement needed?

Is dearer necessarily better?

One of the most dangerous myths is that better quality of service always
costs money. Firms that charge hefty fees just because they are perceived
as 'quality consultants' are not uncommon. They base their aggressive
pricing policies on the same myth – the better, the dearer. Beware of
dealing with these operators.

When a consulting company purchases and installs a new computer
system which runs faster, more efficient and more powerful software and
is capable of acting as an expert system, they may justify higher rates on
the basis of such expensive, advanced equipment. But, on the other hand,
reason tells us: 'Hey, something doesn't quite sit here. If the system has
those capabilities, that should enable them to do jobs at less cost. If
things are done properly the first time, the money that would otherwise
be spent on changes, modifications, adjustments, revisions and rework
can be saved.' So quality doesn't necessarily cost more. Simply, there is
no general rule where the relationship between quality and price is
concerned. Each case has to be analysed on its own merits.

Activity versus value

Another trap many managers fall into is caused by the confusion
between activity and value. The typical manifestation of this fallacy can
be observed where the scope of consulting services is badly defined and
where consultants, eager to prolong the assignment and maximise the
number of billable hours, do many tasks that are either trivial in nature
or completely unnecessary. A confused client, who sees busy bodies
though not the purpose of all that activity, usually thinks: 'These guys
are really good. They can see the need for all this tedious work and
certainly know what has to be done. I'll leave it to them to decide what
to do.' A fatal mistake.

Sometimes a suspicion may crawl in and a sobering client may start
asking himself whether all those activities are really necessary. Even then,
the fear of being perceived as incompetent, narrow-minded and

uninformed quite often paralyses all further investigation into the issue. Initiative displayed and busyness projected are not always what clients would like them to be. Sometimes they are just mimicry tactics to pull the wool over clients' eyes. Buy results, not effort.

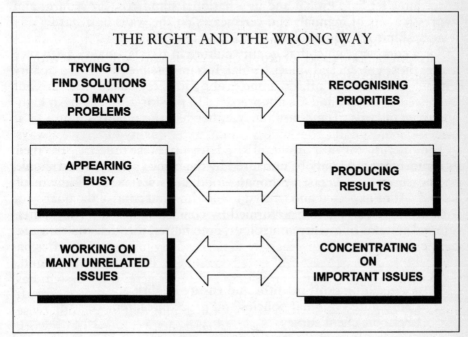

THE RIGHT AND THE WRONG WAY

TRYING TO FIND SOLUTIONS TO MANY PROBLEMS	⟺	RECOGNISING PRIORITIES
APPEARING BUSY	⟺	PRODUCING RESULTS
WORKING ON MANY UNRELATED ISSUES	⟺	CONCENTRATING ON IMPORTANT ISSUES

FIG. 2.1

Talking quality

> It's a funny thing about life, if you refuse to accept anything but the very best you very often get it.
>
> W. Somerset Maugham

Quality, the buzz word of the decade, for so long associated with the manufacturing of products, is increasingly affecting service providers, consulting firms amongst them. One of the developments resulting from the widespread push towards standardisation and uniformisation of quality standards is accreditation or certification. It is a formal recognition, by a national or international accreditation body, that a particular company confirms to a set of procedural standards known as the ISO9000 standards. They specify the rules and norms under which accredited companies should operate and document their actions.

Having a quality assurance scheme does not, however, guarantee the best product at the lowest price. It doesn't mean that a firm's management system is working properly, it doesn't say anything about the quality of people, their knowledge, experience and performance. It simply means that a company is following certain administrative procedures set by national and international standards. Procedures and impressive sets of manuals and certificates on the walls bear hardly any relationship to the quality of the work done.

For a company which has quality culture in praxis, quality assurance makes those entrenched values formal. It is impossible to switch a quality control system on or off, do some grubby jobs for clients who are not interested in quality and are not prepared to pay for it, and some at high-quality standards. The consultancy either has the quality culture or it hasn't.

The quality of a consultant's advice and the success of their assignments should only be measured by the results achieved and should be measured by clients. Although good consultants do, individuals should not be expected and trusted to monitor and control the quality of their work. That is better performed by consulting firms, through their internal systems of quality control, or, even better, through constant and tight client control.

How consulting firms monitor and ensure quality
- ❏ Formalised internal policies and procedures in place
- ❏ Periodic client surveys
- ❏ Feedback from clients during assignments
- ❏ Internal discussions and criticisms
- ❏ Detailed quality control systems
- ❏ External quality audits

Accounting for time

Every consulting company holds its empoyees accountable for their time. Some give their staff monthly budgets they have to meet, usually expressed as a number of hours for which clients can be billed. Some even divide days into six-minute blocks and consultants have to record what they have done with each segment. Law firms are notorious in the use of these 'constant pressure' methods.

You may say, 'There is nothing wrong with keeping them on their toes. This just means that they will work harder for their salaries and bring more benefits to both their employer and their clients.' It simply doesn't work that way. Yes, it will bring some benefits, but only to the consulting company, not to you, the client. All you can be sure of is that they will use every opportunity to maximise their billings and charge you for every second of their time, regardless of the fact that a big chunk of it was spent on activities of no value to you.

Big versus small – the eternal dilemma

With regard to size, consultants can be classified into three broad categories – individuals or freelancers; small firms who usually specialise in certain areas; and big, multidisciplinary firms. This division is very questionable, for there are many small firms, even individuals, who claim they can deal with any aspect of clients' operations (hard to believe), and there are some big firms who specialise in just a few of those aspects.

This brings us to one of the fundamental questions many managers face – which consulting firms are best equipped to handle certain tasks? Most firms state their expertise in very broad terms and claim they can handle almost everything. While this is obviously not true for many small, backyard operators, the issue becomes clouded when big consultancies are in question.

Although some jobs could be done quicker and cheaper by smaller, more specialised firms, which don't charge such high premiums as their bigger brothers, conservative managers are more likely to give the majority or even all their work to big players, with whom they have had an ongoing businss relationship for years.

Small consulting firms and individuals are obviously more flexible and adaptable than big firms. An individual answers only to himself and to his client. Nobody forces upon him a three-volume corporate policy manual, asks him to submit budgets and plans and to reach quotas of billable hours. His ideas, methods and proposals go directly to his clients. Nobody vetoes them or introduces compromises.

Competency, unfortunately, doesn't follow the same logic as flexibility and adaptability. Although it is true that large consulting firms are, due to their size, likely to be inefficient, small firms are not necessarily more efficient. They can be as incompetent as their larger brothers, which is one of the reasons many of them never grow to be big and often become bankrupt.

How can some consulting firms prosper despite low rates?

As we have seen, bigger is not necessarily better. By the same token, cheaper isn't necessarily inferior. Some consultants charge rates which are significantly lower than those of their competitors of comparative reputation and capabilities. This in turn enables them to consistently beat their more expensive rivals and win contracts. The simple secret is that their expenses are much lower; their payroll expenses, overheads, taxes, everything. How is that possible? you may ask. Through the use of 'just-in-time' consulting teams.

No fixed expenses or permanent employees! Individuals are employed on projects when they are needed and kept on them for as long as they are needed. A project team gets formed, does the job and disappears. The secret is in the people employed. They come from various pools: unemployed professionals and managers, retirees, moonlighters and part-time income seekers.

All these categories of people are willing to accept lower rates for work that normally commands higher ones. Unemployed professionals and managers have to eat. Retirees want to keep working, otherwise they feel useless and half-dead. Moonlighters and freelancers are sometimes desperate to get a job; consulting can be a famine. Part-time income seekers are after exactly that – part-time income – and the issue of hourly rates is not of primary importance to them. Any additional income is welcome. Needy or simply greedy, they all want one thing – money.

Comparing proposals and quotes

Spreadsheets are very useful and widely used tools in making objective and fact-based comparisons as the basis of the selection process. These software packages make data entry, comparison and presentation easy and effective. The figures, timing, number of personnel, project phases and anything else of importance can be tabulated or presented in graph form to management and can serve as a record of a proper and thorough selection execise.

Make this your philosophy: never accept the lowest bid without an adequate analysis of the consultants' experience, capability and quality. Many projects and assignments done by the cheapest bidders have gone substantially over budget, resulted in poor quality, in work that has had to be redone, and have taken significantly longer to complete than initially planned. A price tag has no meaning unless it's attached to other aspects of a consulting firm, aspects that can be measured, evaluated, compared, or, as sometimes proves just as accurate, felt.

CONSULTANT EVALUATION AND COMPARISON SHEET

	Consultant 1	Consultant 2	Consultant 3	Consultant 4
Responsiveness				
Quality of documents				
Capability statement				
Professionalism				
References				
Past dealings				
Experience				
Quality of questions asked				
Availability				
Cultural fit				
Fee Schedule				
Likeability				

FIG. 2.2

Probing deeper, aiming higher

Ask for scenarios
A good practice in evaluating consultants and their plans and proposals is to ask for two cases – 'the best case' and 'the worst case' scenarios. Get them to define what they think those two opposite outcomes will be. Make them estimate the likelihood of both outcomes and propose the steps they would take to prevent the worst case scenario from happening. Ask for the risk assessment and what factors may contribute to that downside risk. If they tell you there is no real risk involved, look for another consultant.

Analyse what they say about themselves

Many consulting firms, particularly the bigger ones, regularly produce two types of promotional material. Brochures profiling the company communicate the basic corporate mission statement and credentials to potential clients, while longer, more detailed and elaborate capability statement documents, which are normally available on request or are delivered as part of fee proposal or tender, provide details of past accomplishments, clients, personnel and in-house expertise.

For an individual consultant, a capability brochure is simply an expanded and detailed functional cv. For a consulting firm, it's a booklet that represents the firm and conveys its ability to produce results. In both cases it enhances the consultant's image and visibility, promotes their services (since clients usually file them for future reference), and provides a tangible representation of otherwise intangible qualities.

What can be found in capability brochures?

- ❑ Field consulting firm is in – engineering, training, management consulting, accounting, etc.
- ❑ Specific services the firm provides.
- ❑ Firm's resources, human and material.
- ❑ Summary descriptions of past projects, usually with reference names.
- ❑ Short overview of firm's philosophy, mission statement and quality and business policies.

Qualifying consulting firms merely on the basis of their capability statements and corporate brochures is a very difficult and risky selection method. The glossy brochures, full of beautiful pictures of smiling, satisfied clients, always contain the same platitudes, and should be used only as a base for more detailed investigations. They are designed to create a warm, cosy feeling that bonds the firm with prospective clients and should be taken for what they really are – promotional and advertising material. They may or may not have anything to do with the firm's real capabilities and reputation.

Apart from analysing these corporate brochures and capability statements and documents in depth, all credentials, references and claims should be checked by talking to previous clients and the consultants themselves.

Most clients have a preconceived notion that consultants won't welcome these qualifying investigations and will disclose as little information as possible. The truth is quite different. Business is hard to get, and firms are willing to impart a surprisingly substantial amount of information just to increase their chances of adding a new name to their client list. In many cases even confidential information is revealed, and they often tend to divulge more details than inquiring clients really require at that stage.

Mental exercise
Two types of consultants will approach you looking for assignments. The first type are frank. They will say: 'You have problems that we can help you solve. You are weak in our area of specialisation and need our services.'

The second type have a different approach: 'Your organisation is doing a terrific job. We think we can help you in your achievements. We like your cause and want to play a part in the action.'

Which one would you hire?

Look for signs of trouble

❑ *Short-term focus*. There are two fundamentally different approaches taken by consulting firms in solving problems. 'Short-sighted' operators focus on a certain problem without getting involved in related issues and long-term strategies and plans. The name of the game is to isolate a problem and solve it, without much disturbance to the system and without involvement in the broader view. This type of consultant does what their clients tell them to do and seldom displays initiative in recognising other inadequacies and drawing the client's attention to them. Consultants who keep in mind that repetitive business is good business usually use the long-term approach. While working on the client's immediate needs they also keep an eye on the interrelated and interdependent issues and point them out to the client.

❑ *Morale problems*. In this age of dividing and diminishing loyalties, consulting firms, just like any other companies, may suffer from a lack of dedication, enthusiasm and commitment on the part of their employees. A consulting firm is only as good as the people who work for it. While busy solving their clients' problems, consulting companies quite often suffer from the same ailments, and it's usually the clients who end up paying for inefficiencies, sloppiness and lack of dedication.

❑ *Inconsistencies*. Despite their commitment to client service and to delivering quality results, even reputable consulting firms occasionally turn out a shoddy job, well below their and their clients' standards. No matter how tightly the internal workings of a firm are controlled and how well the projects are managed, don't forget that the law of averages and Murphy's law are at work here. Many clients make a fundamental mistake in assuming that a reputable name on the report guarantees meaningful results.

❑ *Conflicting interests or lack of manpower.* Find out what the consultant's workload is, in particular if they are currently working on several concurrent projects which may lead to internal and external conflicts in terms of commitment, divided loyalties, resources and logistics.

❑ *Desperation.* Avoid consultants who routinely or desperately tender for assignments. Look for ones with rigorous vetting procedures in determining which jobs to bid on.

❑ *Lack of commitment.* Many clients I've spoken to complain that the thing that angers and frustrates them most with some consultants (no matter how capable they may be) is the lack of prompt response and dedication to the client's concerns. Some consultants use the same excuse as the builder who takes a long time to get back to his clients claiming that he has to deal with a dozen projects at the same time. As far as a client is concerned, the consultant is undertaking not only the most important, but, in the client's mind, the only project – his.

❑ *Small signs that mean big trouble.* Dishonesty, lying, unethical behaviour, arrogance, aggressiveness, timidity, lack of drive or enthusiasm, emotional instability, inability to keep promises and appointments, not following the instructions or agreed course of action.

Establish your own data base of consultants

If you or your company haven't had many contacts with consultants in the past, or should you want to expand your list of consulting companies that could be used for future assignments, there are quite a few ways of compiling such a list, which is the first step towards building new business relationships. Sources include:

❑ *Business contacts, friends and acquaintances.* Your business contacts could provide you with detailed information on consulting firms they have used in the past or are using at the moment. They will know each consultant's corporate games, plans and operational methods, so, depending on the nature of your relationship with them, could dispense some information to you. Always foster good relationships with your former employers, customers, suppliers, etc. You never know when you are going to need them.

Friends and relatives can also provide you with specific, 'inside' information about companies they work for, or through them you can meet people who work for the consulting companies you are interested in.

❑ *Business and trade magazines and publications.* Time spent in a library could prove to be a good investment in the information-gathering process. Trade and financial magazines and publications are an excellent source of information. Annual reports, brochures, pamphlets and newsletters published by consulting firms can also be valuable to potential clients.

The Consulting Firm Evaluation Questionnaire

Services provided by the consulting company:
- ❑ What type of services does the company provide?
- ❑ Which areas are the most profitable or have the greatest potential?
- ❑ How are the services provided? What methods are used?
- ❑ Has the firm got quality accreditation? What quality control techniques are used?

Firm's clients and markets:
- ❑ Who are the company's main clients?
- ❑ How good is the relationship between the company and its clients?
- ❑ What is the history of that relationship? What are the present and future trends?
- ❑ What are the firm's plans in the areas of marketing, new markets or expanding the existing ones?

Organisational aspects of the consultancy:
- ❑ How is the company organised? What is the function of each department?
- ❑ How many layers of management does the company have? What are they?
- ❑ What are the main areas of responsibility for each level?
- ❑ Which departments generate profit? Which ones are not so successful?

The firm's history and future plans:
- ❑ When was the company established?
- ❑ Does the company show steady growth over the years?
- ❑ Is the company expanding its business or stagnating?
- ❑ Who are the major shareholders (if the company is listed on the stock market)?

❑ *Associations and institutions.* Every profession has its own professional body or institution which prescribes the rules with which members must comply, a code of ethics and conduct, necessary qualifications and other requirements, and, in some cases, even fee structures. Although membership of these associations is by no means protection from being taken for a ride, it certainly adds to the credibility and reputation of potential consultants. Shoddy backyard operators don't go to that much trouble, and, if they did, most wouldn't be accepted. Or would they?

❑ *Nationally and internationally known consulting firms.* Many clients in need of consulting services are intimidated and frightened off by names such as James McKinsey & Company or Booz, Allen & Hamilton, Inc. They may be expensive, but at least their reputations should serve as a guarantee that you won't be taken advantage of. Furthermore, they have the expertise and know-how to handle complex and sensitive issues which many smaller and lesser-known firms couldn't successfully deal with.

❑ *Advertised invitations to register their interest with your company.* Some companies use this method very effectively. A small advertisement in major national newspapers will attract attention from prospective consultants. Compared with the benefits of maintaining an updated and accurate list and requesting capability statements from twenty or so firms, the cost of these advertisements is negligible.

❑ *Consultants' registers.* These are maintained in order to provide ready access to information on various firms, to promote competition amongst them (for the benefit of clients) and to ensure that individual firms and consultants do not get a disproportionate share of consulting assignments and contracts.

ACME MANUFACTURING CO.

CONSULTANT REGISTER

Acme Manufacturing Company maintains a Register of Consultants as the main reference source from which management, accounting and engineering consultants are selected and invited to tender, undertake studies or provide expert advice.

Professional consulting firms, groups and individual specialists with particular skills, qualifications or experience are invited to register their interest, or confirm or update their current registration with the Company.

The expression of interest should not exceed twelve (12) pages in length and should outline:

❏ Relevant projects and experience
❏ Staff skills and qualifications
❏ References
❏ Areas of expertise

For further information or clarification please contact
. . . .
Registrations should be submitted by . . . .
to the address below:
. . . .

Smart move
Establish your own databank on major consulting companies in your field. Collect articles from newspapers and magazines and other printed materials. Establish a filing system for easy reference and updating.

Chapter 3: Management of Consulting Projects

This is not a book on project management. However, a brief general overview of project management discipline is necessary for the understanding of consulting projects and for maximising your benefits from them. In addition to these basics, some issues should be dealt with in greater detail, due to their impact on the success or failure of projects and client-consultant relationships.

The four cornerstones of a consulting project

Time

> 'Twenty thousand pounds!' cried Sullivan. 'Twenty thousand pounds, which you would lose by a single accidental delay!'
> 'The unforeseen doesn't exist,' quietly replied Phileas Fogg.
> 'But, Mr Fogg, eighty days are only the estimate of the least possible time in which the journey can be made.'
> 'A well-used minimum suffices for everything.'
>
> Jules Verne, *Around the World in Eighty Days*

'Time is life,' said Alan Lakein in his book *How to Get Control of Your Time and Your Life*. 'It is irreversible and irreplaceable. To waste your time is to waste your life, but to master your time is to master your life and make the most out of it.' This is what managing consultants is basically all about: making the most of available time, resources, information and skills.

Time is never cheap, but it is much more so at the beginning of a project. As the project progresses, it becomes more and more expensive. The earlier the planning and control starts, the easier it is to control both budget and quality. This is a fundamental project equation.

A sense of timing is of paramount importance in the business of managing consultants. Your success or failure will more often be determined by the timing of your actions and decisions than by the quality and nature of those actions.

Budget

Budgeting is a tough task simply because it involves predicting the future. Before any project starts, reliable and correct estimates of the associated costs have to be produced. Various levels of estimating accuracy reflect the methods used for their preparation and the level and degree of detail of the available information at the time of their preparation.

There are many kinds of estimates, but the most commonly used classification is based on the degree of accuracy:

- ❑ Order of magnitude estimate (+/- 30%)
- ❑ Preliminary estimate (+/- 20%)
- ❑ Definitive estimate (+/- 10%)
- ❑ Detailed estimate (+/- 5%)

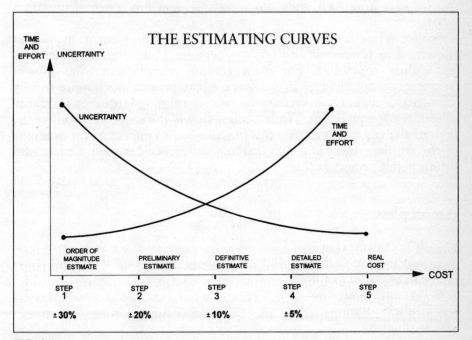

FIG. 3.1

For budgeting purposes the order of magnitude estimate is used. Once the project is approved and preliminary work has been carried out, the preliminary estimate can be done. The definitive estimate and the detailed estimate are available only after extensive work, when the project is well and truly under way and the definition, investigation and data-gathering phases have been carried out.

Quality

How do we define quality? It depends on the vantage point. Your definition may not necessarily be the same as your consultant's. To you, the client, quality is not the consulting firm's quality standards and accreditation. It is the fulfilment of your standards and expectations, doing jobs right the first time, and doing them right every time afterwards.

Scope

The scope of a consulting project is the set of tasks, activities and services that will have to be performed and delivered during the life of a project. If time says when and for how long, if costs say for how much, and if quality says how well, then scope answers the fundamental question: what?

Project scope is the fourth variable in the project equation, just as important as time, cost and quality, yet somehow often neglected and less tightly controlled. For some reason, many clients and project managers accept changes in the scope of the project much more readily than they accept cost overruns, the project running late or poor quality of services or equipment. While 'scaling down' the scope may well be the least of all evils, in some cases this practice has an impact on the outcome of the whole project and may make a difference between a successful solution and project failure.

Project phases

1. Project definition
2. Information-gathering and selection
3. Analysis and synthesis
4. Recommendations
5. Implementation
6. Evaluation
7. Completion and closure – disengagement

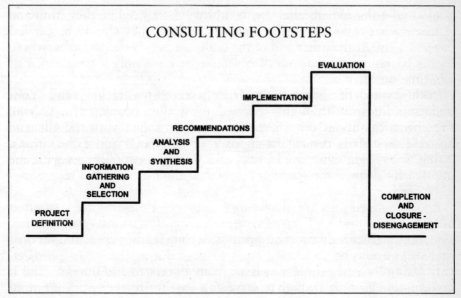

FIG. 3.2

Project Definition

Well begun is half done. – Horace

One of the key strategies for proper management of consultants is to get them to focus on a problem that is clearly and simply postulated. Stating the facts and clarifying the issues is your task. Don't make the very common mistake of delegating it to a consultant. More often than not managers merely say: 'We have a problem with so and so. Tell me what's wrong and what can be done about it.' Although that's exactly what consultants should be doing, they obviously need much more information to get started. To provide them with that information is your first task. Narrow the focus down, otherwise they'll go out at all tangents, tackling a myriad issues and charging you for significantly more hours than is really necessary.

Defining the problem or issues the project should concentrate on sounds like a trivial first phase. The truth is that most projects fail at that very first step and so begin without proper definition. Assignments where consultants start work with a very vague idea of what the client is trying to achieve are very common.

Consulting assignments vary widely in terms of scope, aims, methods used and approach to problems. They also vary in terms of the client's knowledge and definition. At one end of the spectrum are highly structured jobs, where the clients know exactly what they want to achieve, what tasks have to be performed, how they should be carried out and why. At the other end of the scale are poorly defined jobs, where clients barely know the overall objective or have only a rough idea of what the problem is.

Both types of assignments can create frustration and mis-understandings. With highly defined jobs, the consultant may have different ideas about certain aspects, and a conflict with the client is possible unless the consultant chooses simply to carry out the client's instructions unequivocally. In that case, all responsibility lies with the client, who defined the scope and specified the methods and techniques to be used.

Poorly defined jobs are much more common. Problems are very often hidden, buried under a heap of symptoms, manifestations, related issues, contributing factors, false assumptions, wrong leads, personal opinions, prejudices and egos.

Isolating the real problem or issue from all related and unrelated junk and defining it firmly enough to serve as a base for further work is not an easy task. That is probably the reason why so many clients leave it to the consultant.

When consultants have freedom in defining their assignments, they either imitate each other or simply repeat one of the previous assignments of a similar kind, just with a higher price tag. This very common 'standard package' plot is a recipe for failure for both clients and consultants.

Defining a problem – problem statement

Only well-defined problems can be solved successfully. A good problem statement should always be your first step towards finding a solution. The paths that lead to a good problem statement differ. You can arrive at it yourself and then incorporate your definition in your brief to the consultant, who will then use it as the basis for his assignment. You can define a problem together with the consultant, or you can provide only the outline of the problem or issue and make it the consultant's first task to investigate and produce a problem statement. No matter which approach you choose to use, a good problem statement is mandatory for success. A good problem statement:

❑ Focuses on the effects, not the causes – that comes later
❑ Quantifies the problem in some way – how much, how often, for how long, since when, etc.
❑ Includes only facts, not feelings, speculations, options – what, where, when are the key questions

❏ Measures the deficiency (the difference between the results that are desired and the present situation)
❏ Avoids implying solutions – this comes later

Before dealing with a problem, always clear your mind of old prejudices, biases, ideas or feelings. Start afresh. Take nothing for granted and don't automatically handle the issue the same way similar ones were handled in the past. And always do two things:

1. Be excited about the challenge and the opportunity to find a solution
2. Assume that solution can and will be found: it is just a matter of time

---

Problem Analysis – the Questions
Both as a starting point in your problem definition and analysis, and as a permanent monitoring tool, some questions should constantly be asked along the way:

❏ What are my alternatives? What are the pros and cons of each alternative?
❏ What developments could affect my mission?
❏ What knowledge and skills will I need to successfully complete my mission?
❏ Where and how do I acquire the knowledge and develop the skills needed?
❏ How will my choices affect my future?
❏ What are the critical factors of my success?
❏ How do I control and achieve those critical factors?

Information-gathering and selection

❏ *Data sources*

> *Research is simply the manner in which men solve the knotty problems in their attempt to push back the frontiers of human ignorance.*
> Paul D. Leedy, *Practical Research: Planning and Design*

Many mistakes consultants make can be traced down to incomplete, inaccurate or outdated information. Information-gathering is always a crucial step in problem-solving, and it is probably the reason why so many consultants overdo it. That uneasy feeling that something has been forgotten or overlooked, or that some individuals who may have valuable information were not talked to, is always present in the minds of 'the foot soldiers'. The worst that can happen is that their seniors may discover that something has been left out.

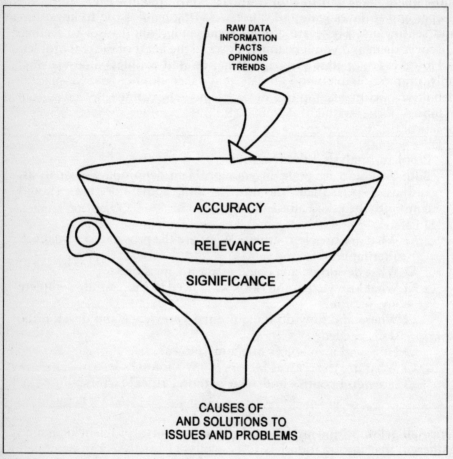

RAW DATA
INFORMATION
FACTS
OPINIONS
TRENDS

ACCURACY

RELEVANCE

SIGNIFICANCE

CAUSES OF
AND SOLUTIONS TO
ISSUES AND PROBLEMS

FIG. 3.3

❏ Summarising and selection

There are no facts, only interpretations.

Friedrich Nietzsche

While gathering, sorting and analysing data, it may be worthwhile to write short summaries at regular intervals. The summaries help to outline the known facts, distil them, separate the key points and issues and provide guidance in making decisions about where further analysis is needed.

Separate facts from feelings. Some managers go to extremes and completely discard feelings, opinions, hunches and intuition. By concentrating on qualitative, irrefutable facts and turning a blind eye to those qualitative elements, they, in effect, fail to follow leads, to explore deeper and to investigate the causes and origins of those feelings, fears and sentiments. There are always some underlying causes to feelings. Discover them and you'll be much closer to the heart of the real problem.

However, once past the data-gathering and problem-analysis stage, only unquestionable, undoubted, real facts should have a place in definition documents, reports and implementation plans. Perceived facts, assumed facts, wished-for facts and other apparent facts have no practical use, because they aren't facts at all.

Data sources include:

- ❏ Interviews with employees, customers, suppliers, contractors and other consultants
- ❏ Standards, specifications, briefs, scopes of work, reports, memos
- ❏ Personal observations, knowledge and experience
- ❏ Books, magazines, newsletters, product reviews, manuals, instruction books
- ❏ Alarm printouts, log books, recorded measurements
- ❏ Photographs, graphs and charts

Analysis and synthesis

> Not everything that counts can be counted, and not everything that can be counted counts.
>
> Sir George Pickering, often quoted by Albert Einstein

Once all relevant and useful information about a problem or issue is gathered, that information has to be analysed. Analysis can be done in many ways, but there are two distinguished methods: qualitative, which studies the issues, causes and consequences, and the dependencies and relations between them; and quantitative, which analyses proportions, trends and numerical representations of the reality.

Analysis is not an end, its chief objective is to find causes of problems. It is only a prelude to synthesis, whose main aim is to develop and apply solutions to those problems.

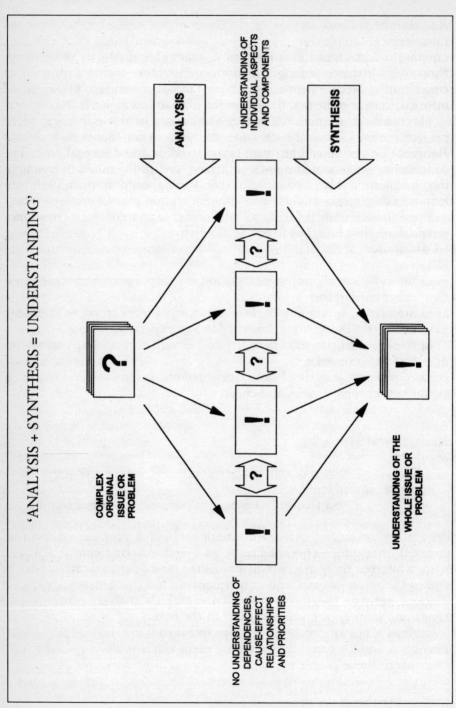

FIG. 3.4

Recommendations

In a typical consulting assignment, recommendations are the first tangible results consultants have to deliver. This is usually done in the form of a written report, which not only presents clients with a set of consultant's recommendations, but also provides background information about how those recommendations were arrived at.

This justification starts with the methods used in previous stages of the project (definition, data-gathering, analysis). Then the report should elaborate on the consultant's findings based on the data gathered. The conclusions made would also be analysed, giving a detailed overview of the consultant's way of thinking and reasoning, supported with relevant facts and case studies.

Recommendations tell the client what *that particular consultant* would do in his place. It doesn't necessarily mean that it is the right thing to do. Recommendations are not to be accepted indiscriminately and followed blindly, as many clients do. They are simply a basis for further evaluation by the client, or more often, by both client and consultant. Only after a detailed assessment of those recommendations and an appraisal of their viability and practicality should they be put into practice.

Making unrealistic recommendations is probably the most common mistake by consultants at this stage and a continuous source of complaints from frustrated clients. This is obviously where a consultant's experience, practicality and intimate knowledge of the client's organisation, its capabilities and restrictions comes into the equation. A recommended solution that is feasible and applicable in one client's environment may well be totally unacceptable or unworkable in another's.

Working out the details

A grasshopper, having survived two harsh and long winters, turned to a wise owl for help. The owl listened silently to the grasshopper's story and then suggested a solution to his problem: 'It's all relatively simple. All you should do is turn yourself into a cricket and then you'll be able to hibernate through the next winter.'

The grasshopper went merrily on his way, full of gratitude towards the old owl. A couple of days later, the grasshopper returned. 'You didn't tell me how to perform the metamorphosis into a cricket. 'Look,' said the owl, 'I gave you the principle, you'll have to work out the details yourself.'

From *Clients and Consultants* by Chip R. Bell and Leonard Nadler. Copyright © 1985 by Gulf Publishing Company, Houston, TX. Used with permission. All rights reserved.

Implementation

> *If to do were as easy as to know what were good to do, chapels had been churches and poor men's cottages princes' palaces.*
>
> William Shakespeare

From the manager's point of view the big disadvantage of the consulting approach to problem-solving is that people who make recommendations (consultants) are not always responsible for the 'finished product' – the implementation of those recommendations. The responsible ones are the managers themselves. It's always a good policy to include the task of implementation in a consultant's brief. If you want to be left out in the cold with a couple of reports and recommendations, fine. If not, you had better make sure those recommendations are put into practice.

This can be done by your employees under the consultant's supervision and with his assistance, or by the consultant's personnel, without involvement from your people.

The first path is obviously more beneficial to you. Firstly, employees involved in the exercise will assume the ownership of the project, as a direct consequence of their active involvement. They won't perceive change as something imposed on them, but something they created and brought to life. This fact alone makes it much more likely that the whole project will be successful.

Secondly, through their participation, members of your team will gain valuable experience, which could prove useful to both themselves and the organisation. At a later date, should a similar issue arise again, they would be able to call on their newly gained skills and save you time and money in consultant's fees.

Evaluation

> *To err is human. To forgive is not this company's policy.*
>
> Anonymous sign to company's consultants

The evaluation of consulting projects takes two forms. The ongoing evaluation is a continuous process which takes place during the whole life of a project. The final evaluation is carried out before the project is closed and is usually recorded in a document that may be called 'Final Project Report' or 'Final Report'.

Once the consultant's recommendations are implemented, clients normally carry out the evaluation of the whole project and, if possible, the results achieved. Evaluation of the results and benefits may not be possible at such an early stage due to the fact that the final effect of consultation may require several months or a couple of years to become obvious and measurable. If that is the case, at least the evaluation methods and criteria for assessment of the results should be agreed on between client and consultant.

Evaluating The Evaluation Process
- ❏ What has to be evaluated?
- ❏ Why does it have to be evaluated?
- ❏ Who will do the measurement and how often?
- ❏ How are the results going to be measured?
- ❏ Is the evaluation process going to be cost-effective? How much will it cost?
- ❏ Who will do the evaluation, how and when?
- ❏ Who is going to see the results of evaluation and what action is he going to take?

Evaluation serves several very important purposes. Firstly, it reassures the client by justifying the time, effort and expenses incurred during the project and by emphasising the tangible benefits that are a direct or indirect result of the consultant's actions. Secondly, it serves as an educational exercise for the client and supports his professional growth by enabling him to learn from the experiences gained. Thirdly, it provides the consultant with feedback on his performance, which will lead to corrective actions on similar tasks in the future and provide the consultant with a sense of accomplishment and satisfaction.

Some consultants will be unwilling to have their work evaluated. Their usual excuse is along the lines of 'my work is so complex and involved it cannot possibly be evaluated'. This reluctance is a danger sign and a reason for caution.

The final evaluation					
What	Consultant's performance	Client's performance	Project plan versus actuals	Achieved results	Difficulties encountered
How	Observation, discussion	Observation, discussion	Comparison	Measurement	Records, discussion
Why	To enable consultants to improve their performance and provide better service in future.	To enable clients to improve their performance and manage better on future projects.	To evaluate the planning and estimating process.	To determine the success of the whole project.	To prepare to deal with them, should the same issues arise in the future.

Measuring results is the final and most important step of every evaluation process and the whole project. This is the time to ask yourself some hard questions and to try to find the answers.

❑ Was the project completed on time and within budget? If not, why not?
❑ Has the scope of the project changed during its life? What were the reasons for that change?
❑ How much has your organisation learned while working with a consultant?
❑ How would you assess the quality, appropriateness and completeness of the final project report?
❑ Would you engage the same consultant again?

There is no right or wrong way to evaluate consulting projects and measure the achieved results. Based on proven principles and fundamentals of evaluation, both consultants and clients have to establish the evaluation systems which will best suit their circumstances.

Project Closure Notice
❑ Project name and number; closure date
❑ The reason for closure (completion, lack of funds, cancellation of the job, etc.)
❑ Special instructions on the outstanding tasks that are to be finished
❑ Distribution list

Completion and closure – disengagement

Everything has its beginning and end, and consulting projects are no exception. Just as signing a contract or an agreement may be the official start of a project, so it is important that the end of a project be marked by a formal closure. The project closure notice should be issued to all concerned and involved parties, including your company's accounting department and the consultants who performed the work. This will minimise the chance of further man-hours being booked to the project, but will still allow processing of late invoices and help to tie up a few loose ends.

Smart Move
Some less scrupulous consultants try to keep booking a few hours
here and there to projects that have been closed, but where the
official notice hasn't been received from the client. Beware of that
practice and notify them officially that the project is closed and
further billable hours will not be accepted!

Planning and Scheduling

> *'Living backwards!' Alice repeated in great astonishment. 'I
> never heard of such a thing.'*
>
> *'—but there's one great advantage in it, that one's memory
> works both ways.'*
>
> *'I'm sure mine only works one way,' Alice remarked. 'I
> can't remember things before they happen.'*
>
> *'It's a poor sort of memory that only works backwards,' the
> Queen remarked.*
>
> Lewis Carroll, *Through the Looking-Glass*

Events usually don't happen according to our plans and projections, and
the reality almost always differs to some extent from our tidy and
logically organised plans and models. Thoughtful planning, though, no
matter how simplified it may be, is still essential as a monitoring and
controlling tool.

Structured approach to tasks, assignments and projects
A structured approach to project management and problem-solving is
dictated by two factors. The first is the size and complexity of a project.
The more involved and complex a project is, the more necesssary a
structured approach is. The second factor is the requirement for success.
A structured approach is essential in project management.

What is a structured approach? It is a systematic, logical, organised,
disciplined, planned, monitored and managed way of applying
knowledge, experience and effort towards achieving the goals of the
project.

The breakdown of work that has to be done should simultaneously be
analysed from two opposite perspectives. A top-down approach should
be used to detail the tasks and identify the key deliverables and
milestones which can easily be understood, estimated and controlled. A
bottom-up approach should be used to ensure that individuals and teams
have identified all the tasks they have to perform.

Smart move
Attend courses on project management, planning and budgeting, and problem-solving. Read books covering the same topics. A good start would be D. Lock, *Project Management*. Those three topics are fundamental to dealing with consultants. Then read this book again.

Matrix approach to project teams

Many consultants use the so-called matrix project form, which is centred around entire projects rather than being fixed around separate organisational functions performed by departments such as marketing, sales, design, construction, distribution, accounting, engineering, etc.

Each team member has his role and place in the matrix. A flexible matrix is important to a client, because a third party or client's own employees can easily be integrated into the structure.

Another useful aspect of matrix structure is its ease of graphical presentation in a two-dimensional form. That simple matrix, where functions or levels in organisation are listed across the top row and project activities down the left column, is used to estimate the workload per task and/or per functional level, from which an estimate of the consultant's costs can be made.

The cause, not the effect!

> 'What does the fish remind you of?'
> 'Other fish.'
> 'And what do other fish remind you of?'
> 'Other fish.'
>
> Joseph Heller, *Catch 22*

Books are read from the beginning to the end. Projects are managed, problems solved and businesses run the opposite way. One starts at the end, with project goals, problem definition or business mission statement, and then moves towards realisation of what has to be done to reach the end.

Paperwork and documentation

Request for a proposal or tender

An invitation for tenders given by a prospective client to consultants is merely an invitation to negotiate with those who reply, and not, as some consultants expect, an offer to enter into a contractual arrangement with a consultant whose quote is the lowest, or with any consultant at all. It should be treated (by both parties) merely as an exercise whose aim is to ascertain whether project costs will be prohibitive or whether they will enable a client to pursue the matter further.

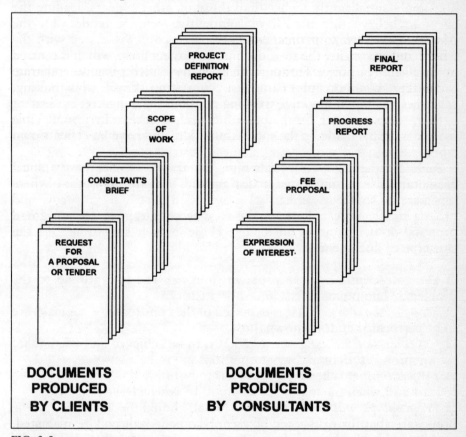

FIG. 3.5

Most clients, however, with every right to do so, draft their invitations in such a way as to obtain firm offers, upon which a binding contract can be based. The cost of tendering is the consultant's responsibility, and a client will not be liable for the expenses involved unless it can be shown that he had no intention of giving the contract to the consultant in question or to any of those invited for tender. This lack of intention would make the whole process fraudulent and bidding consultants would be entitled to recover their expenses in the form of damages paid by the client. Beware of that fact! An invitation to tender is a legal document. Submitting a bid constitutes a consultant's acceptance of the terms outlined in the tender documents, and forms a legally binding contract.

Some consultants, rather than declining an offer to tender and facing the risk of damaging their relations with an inviting client, put forward tenders, submissions or proposals which are not genuine. Those tenders are simply significantly higher than those of other bidders, leading the client to believe that they have competitive genuine tenders for the project. The consultant thus avoids the high costs associated with the tender and maintains the relationship, displaying good will and interest in the client's business. This practice is legally called collusive tendering.

Another common plot amongst consulting firms who have a constructive and cooperative working relationship is a secret agreement between two or more firms not to bid against each other. Some even share the profits made by the successful bidder and have 'my clients' and 'your clients'.

Such a practice is not unlawful. So if you wonder why some consultants are not interested in dealing with you, the answer is obvious – you are on somebody else's list!

Let's finally take a look at the format of a typical request for a proposal or an invitation for tender. These sections should be found in that type of document:

❑ *Short description of the problem or issue*. The background to the problem. Main points, facts, and short history.
❑ *Scope of the work*. What is expected of the consultant, what tasks are to be performed and, if known, how.
❑ *Objectives of the assignment*. What is to be achieved and why. What information is sought and what questions are to be answered.
❑ *Project timing*. When the project has to be finished, when it is planned to start and when the major stages are to be reached.
❑ *Proposal format and standard*. What should be included in the proposal, what format should be used, how proposals will be evaluated.
❑ *Applicable regulations, laws, standards and contract terms*. Defines the legal framework of the consulting project and the standards and regulations that have to be followed. Serves as a reference in the case of disputes, complaints and variations.

Smart Move
When soliciting proposals from consultants, your message should be: 'Don't stop at explaining your proposal. Sell it to me. Make me buy it by creating a need, by making me understand the benefits and the advantages it may have over other proposals and methods.'

Consultants' briefs

In many cases problems happen because the consultant does not know what he is really supposed to do, so he either does it wrong or doesn't do it at all. It is unfortunate that it is always the consultant who gets blamed in these cases, despite the fact that it is the client who has failed to communicate the requirements clearly and effectively.

After an initial discussion or briefing, ask the consultant to express his views on the issue in question. You could ask for a verbal summary or a written one. It could be a separate document or part of proposal. The delivery is of secondary importance in this case. Clarity, systematic thinking and understanding of concepts is what you are looking for at this stage. If he can't summarise the problem, his view of the situation and his concepts on how to go about it, he probably doesn't understand it. Only if he can explain it in a brief, precise way, can you be sure he knows and understands what the issue is all about. This is your acid test.

Always make the 'due by' date known, either by stating it explicitly in your brief or by emphasising it during the first meeting or briefing session. That way you make the consultant realise how serious you are about the whole business and reassure him that you aren't simply waffling about elusive schemes. A due date makes the assignment look like a project and brings in a note of seriousness and time-consciousness.

The Anatomy of a Good Brief
- ❑ Description of the project and its objectives
- ❑ Consultant's tasks
- ❑ Project timing
- ❑ Critical performance indicators (how will the consultant's performance be measured and evaluated)

Fee proposals and tenders

Although the preparation of a fee proposal or a tender submission sometimes takes days or even weeks, it is normally regarded as a marketing effort on the consultant's part and even consultants don't make a fuss about it. All you have to do is make sure you don't pay for it upfront. It is, however, difficult to avoid paying for it later, for most consultants simply include those preparation and production costs in their overall fee.

The tendering process is increasingly becoming difficult for consultants, due to the fact that costs are staying high and profit margins are shrinking under the pressure of competition. The solution to that problem, which affects clients more than they think, is to organise the tendering and selection process in two stages.

The first stage would be limited to expressions of interest, and thus the consulting firms would need to expend only a limited amount of time and effort. From that list of interested firms, a short list would be compiled and those consultants invited to submit detailed tender documents or proposals.

The benefits for consultants are obvious. Firstly, they don't have to wait a long time to find out whether they have been successful. The cost of uncertainty, especially in larger projects, may be significant, although difficult to measure. Planning, budgeting, forecasting, recruitment are all activities that are affected by long waiting times between the submission of the bid and the award of the contract. It helps in making decisions about keeping the project team together, if the chances of winning the assignment justify the cost of maintaining the team ready to commence negotiations and consultations.

Secondly, if a consultant doesn't make it to the short list, they don't have to formulate a fully costed proposal, which is an expensive and time-consuming exercise.

For clients, the benefits of the two-stage tendering approach are less explicit, but nevertheless substantial. Weeding out firms who are unable to meet the requirements is easier and quicker. Elimination of firms with non-compliant or non-competitive bids is also facilitated. The main benefit, however, comes in terms of flexibility. Once a short list is agreed on, discussions with short-listed firms can begin. The scope of consulting services, anticipated concepts, alternative methods of approach, professional fees and other aspects of the assignment can be discussed, negotiated and changed if necessary.

If the brief for the project is changed substantially as a result of these discussions and negotiations, then all short-listed consultancies have to be asked to adjust their proposals accordingly. In a single-stage tendering, all bidders would have to be invited to resubmit their bids, which would damage the client's credibility and reputation, and increase costs for both the client and the consultants.

So far we have been discussing solicited proposals, where the client initiated the action. Although this is by far the most common type of situation, it isn't uncommon for a consultant to put forward an unsolicited proposal. In such a case a consultant believes he has something of value to offer the client or perceives that the client may need his services, and submits his plans and ideas in proposal form.

An Effective Proposal
- ❏ Reassures the client that the consultant understands the project
- ❏ Communicates the consultant's views on the subject to the client
- ❏ Outlines in a tangible form proposed (usually intangible) services
- ❏ Acts as a starting point for negotiations and justifications
- ❏ Enables client and consultant to establish a closer working relationship
- ❏ Provides an opportunity for the consultant to demonstrate his abilities and expertise

---

What should a properly written fee proposal or tender contain? Which issues should it address? Here is a general checklist:

❏ *Assignment or project objectives.* Specifies what is to be achieved and why the job will be carried out. These are the desired outcomes, the bottom line that the consultant will always have to keep in mind. It defines some major questions that will be asked during the project's life: Why are we doing this? Is it necessary? Is it taking us towards our goal or objective?

❏ *Method of approach.* Clear explanation of how the consultant intends to approach the problem and what steps will be taken on the road towards finding a solution to the problem.

❏ *Critical success factors.* How is the project going to be evaluated? On what assumptions and premises? How will positive (successful) outcomes be defined? What are the negative outcomes? Who is going to measure or evaluate those outcomes and how?

❏ *Key personnel.* Names, qualifications and experience of all senior and other key personnel who will be involved in the project.

❏ *Priorities.* What aspects of the job (project) are more important and which are of lesser significance?

❏ *Major stages and milestones.* How are major project stages defined? When does one stage end and another begin? Which events (milestones) will mark the start and the end of each stage? What deliverables will be associated (expected by the client) with each milestone?

❑ *Specific exclusions*. If there is any aspect, task or phase of the assignment that either the client or the consultant wants to exclude from the contract or the scope of the consulting services, it should be done here. It may encompass both goods and services.

❑ *Client's obligations and duties*. It isn't enough to detail the consultant's duties and tasks. This section should eliminate any doubt about what the client's involvement will be by explicitly stating the support and specific actions that will be undertaken by the client.

❑ *Key deliverables*. What does a consultant have to produce (deliver)? Is it a project report, a complete study, a new installation, a working system or just a concept, in what format, how and when? This section defines the tangible goods a consultant has to produce or the intangible services (ideas, concepts, methods, recommendations) presented in a tangible form (report, study, etc.).

❑ *Third parties, their tasks and obligations*. This section should identify any third parties, other consultants or subcontractors who may be involved in certain phases of the project. It should also specify the nature and approximate length of their involvement.

❑ *Time schedule*. Major phases, tasks and activities should be identified, listed and scheduled with respect to one another, taking into account all dependencies, priorities and logical and efficient sequences of steps.

❑ *Schedule of fees*. Whether the project is to be done on a time and material basis, where all expenses and hours worked will be reimbursed on a fixed-price basis. The applicable hourly, weekly or other rates should be specified here by the consultant.

❑ *Meetings and reporting*. Proposes the frequency and format of progress meetings and interim reports. Also specifies where the meetings are to be held and who is to attend them.

❑ *Termination clause*. Specifies who has the power and the right to terminate the contract, and in what circumstances. Also lists the duties, obligations and entitlements of each party in that case.

The Four Cs of a Winning Proposal

❑ Complete   ❑ Concise   ❑ Clear   ❑ Convincing

Contracts

> *One party generally benefits more than the other from vague*
> *or non-binding language in a contract or letter agreement.*
> *Determine upfront whether a vague agreement or an airtight*
> *one better suits your purpose.*
>
> Mark H. McCormack, *What They Don't Teach You*
> *At Harvard Business School*

A formal, written contract or agreement between a client and consultant
serves two basic purposes. The first is to explicitly and precisely stipulate
the rights, duties and obligations of each party. The second is to serve as
a reference and a bridging instrument should disputes arise. Despite
mutual efforts and good intentions, costs escalate, projects run late,
communication deteriorates and expensive litigations or arbitrations
loom. With a clearly written contract, the disruptive and counterproductive (for everybody except lawyers, naturally) course of litigation
can be avoided. Never sign a contract that doesn't specify exactly what a
consultant has to do, what results have to be produced, by when and how
much that is going to cost you (for fixed-priced contracts) or on what
basis the consultant will be paid (for reimbursable contracts).

Despite the obvious advantages of clear, written arrangements,
contracts can also be verbal, or partly verbal and partly in writing. The
contract is constituted by an offer made by the consultant and accepted
by the client. For such a simple contract to be enforceable, it has to be
supported by consideration or quid pro quo. Consideration simply
means that there has to be an express promise by each party that they
will pay for the work (client) or perform the work (consultant).

The problem with contracts is very simple, yet very difficult to resolve.
With some consultants a detailed contract is a waste of time; you simply
don't need it. They value the client, play fair and deliver what has to be
delivered – the results. With others, an airtight contract is a must. They
'play by the contract' and do only what's printed in black and white; not
an ounce more, not an ounce less. In some cases, this may produce
results. In most cases it doesn't. Stay away from these players.

This brings us to the fundamental problem: how to distinguish
between these two mentalities. How to make sure you deal only with the
first group and avoid the second. The answer is still unknown. If clients
knew it, the good guys would prosper and the bad guys would be out of
business forever. We all know that is not the case. We still have a lot to
learn, and the supply of naive, gullible and reckless clients is abundant.

The main flaw in any contract is lack of flexibility. First, the consultant
is not a mechanic in your local garage. The work is usually difficult to
define in detail and quite often the whole set of premises changes during

the life of a project – fresh information is available, the scope changes, new light is shed on the problem. Priorities shift, new methods or more hours become necessary. Contracts aren't very adaptable and interpretable documents. If they are, they are not good contracts.

Without a contract, consulting fees, the scope or anything else that has to be renegotiated can be changed more easily than when a contract exists. If the client wants to terminate the relationship, for whatever reason, it can be done more simply without a contract than with one. It is always a wise policy to include a suitable termination or variation clause, just in case something goes wrong or changes are needed.

Smart move
It is always very interesting to see what a consulting firm wishes to be included in the contract, because it tells you what they perceive as important. So, if they don't request it explicitly, ask them if there is anything they think should be added to your draft of the contract.

As a general philosophy in business, avoid your company's legal department, unless you deliberately want to stall the whole project. Advise consultants to do the same, as a gesture of goodwill and reciprocity. That way you get your solutions and they get their fees sooner and without hassles. This is just one example of a very powerful philosophy for a client: always help the other side! Why? Because the best projects or assignments are the ones without disputes, misunderstandings and, heaven forbid, lawyers. These dealings need contracts and agreements that are sound, fair and beneficial to both parties. Create win-win situations and you'll go a long way in managing consultants.

What to Include in a Contract?

❏ Time schedule	❏ Arbitration clause
❏ Roles and responsibilities	❏ Ownership of produced
❏ Termination clause	systems, procedures, ideas,
❏ Scope of work	documents, software
❏ Goals and objectives	❏ Schedule of fees
❏ Deliverables	❏ Confidentiality clause
❏ Cancellation policy	❏ Incentives and penalities
	❏ Reporting and communications

A verbal contract isn't worth the paper it's written on.
Samuel Goldwyn (attributed)

Many project managers proclaim that their aim is to have 'tight' contracts. How tight is tight? No contract is as tight as clients would like it to be. It is impossible to think of everything, let alone include it in a contract. Omissions and ambiguities are inevitable and have to be lived with.

There are two distinctive aspects of consulting contracts. The formal side is concerned with technicalities: services to be performed, results to be achieved, methods to be used, time schedule to be adhered to, payment methods. The informal side covers the psychological aspects of the client-consultant relationship.

The inclusion of certain clauses in contracts is always a wise policy. One of them is the right to inspect the consultant's books, records and expense receipts. The other is the penalty clause, where, in the case of fixed price contracts, the consultant has to absorb all cost overruns. If the consultant's performance is unacceptable, a provision that gives the client power to terminate the relationship after a predefined notice will prove of enormous value.

Don't, however, include anything in the contract that you are not prepared to enforce with determination and back up with action. If consultants realise that you are willing to give up one or more of the requirements stated in a contract, they will surely try to elicit further concessions and get away with sloppier and less contract-bound work. Your credibility will be destroyed and corners will be cut.

The Essential Elements of a Contract

❑ *Intention.* The intention of both parties has to be to enter into a legally binding agreement.

❑ *Offer and Acceptance.* The consultant has to inform the client that he's willing to accept the specified terms, and once the client informs the consultant that his offer, tender or fee proposal has been accepted without qualification, the contract becomes legally binding.

❑ *Consideration.* Both parties have to promise the other a substantial and valuable benefit. The consultant promises to perform certain services, while the client promises to accept those services and pay for them.

❑ *Capacity.* The consultant must be capable of performing the tasks and delivering the services offered, otherwise he has no power to make the offer to the client and the contract is void.

Changing and adjusting contracts is necessary in certain cases, usually when either the scope of the work changes or one of the parties is not getting a fair deal. Consultants want to work for understanding and fair clients just as clients want to keep a good consultant. So, if a consultant working for you has to put in far more hours than he originally estimated, consider readjusting the terms and fees. A little flexibility in a case like this will go a long way towards establishing a mutually satisfying business relationship.

Progress reports

Longer assignments usually have the fees organised into regular progress payments. A client is invoiced regularly (usually monthly) for services performed in the previous period. Most consultants automatically send their progress reports together with requests for payment, so clients can see exactly what tasks were worked on, who worked on them and for how many hours, what problems were encountered and what was achieved.

Some consultants, however, send those reports only if explicitly asked to do so or if an agreement, contract or scope of work (whatever the legal document that binds the two parties is called) specifically makes this requirement. Make sure you include a clause requesting regular written progress reports.

Progress reports should include (but not be limited to):

- ❑ Summary of the completed work
- ❑ Estimate of the percentage completed (actual versus total job or planned versus actual)
- ❑ Hours spent and cost for each activity
- ❑ Events and developments affecting the performance, timing or scope of the work performed
- ❑ Miscellaneous issues (industrial relations report, personnel changes, safety/accident report, etc.)

Exception reports

The aim of exception reports is to promptly address issues, problems and concerns that may affect the outcome of the project. These acute concerns usually cannot wait until the next scheduled project meeting or progress report and require immediate attention and resolution by the client. Exception reports are a sensible practice which follows in the footsteps of 'management by exception' and prevents busy clients from being inundated by long and detailed routine reports, filled with less relevant information.

Final reports

Always compare final reports and initial proposals. The less the difference, the better the consultant has kept his promises. Although there are assignments that don't require a final report, it is always a wise policy to request one. Consultants will appreciate it, too, because it will give them a chance to summarise their work, elaborate on their actions and problems encountered and use it as an advertising and selling promotional tool to solidify the business relationship between the two parties.

It isn't enough just to read the final report. No matter how closely you study it, it will be difficult to evaluate the success of the whole assignment. What is needed is a comparison between the initial proposal and the final report. The final report should cover all topics and issues brought up in the proposal and examine them in detail.

Have them side by side on your desk and study them together. Are there are points that were mentioned in the proposal, but not in the report? Are there any issues that were just touched upon lightly, yet warranted a more detailed investigation? Are there any new issues that were not envisaged at the preliminary stage, but were later recognised as important?

Records management

During the course of a project, you'll regularly supply consultants with material of various kinds: reports, studies, brochures, internal and confidential documents, books, listings, databases, software programmes and files. Always make sure they know which items have to be returned after the completion of a project. Mark them with your or your company's name and 'To be returned' in large letters. In addition, make a list of those documents and hand it to a consultant at the closure of a project.

The best policy is to keep all relevant documents, correspondence and other relevant written material in a hardcover project file, divided into suitable sections. This will make it easier to find and store information, and also to archive the file on to a project register once the job is finished.

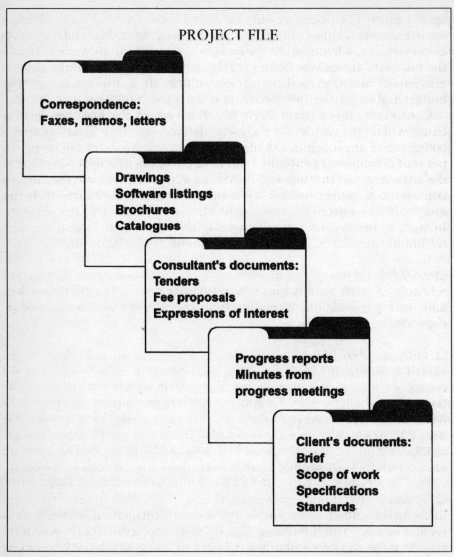

PROJECT FILE

Correspondence:
Faxes, memos, letters

Drawings
Software listings
Brochures
Catalogues

Consultant's documents:
Tenders
Fee proposals
Expressions of interest

Progress reports
Minutes from
progress meetings

Client's documents:
Brief
Scope of work
Specifications
Standards

FIG. 3.6

Financial issues

Types of contracts and payment methods

❑ *Lump sum*. A contract where the consultant agrees to perform tasks specified by the client for a fixed fee are also called 'lump sum' contracts. In normal circumstances, a consultant cannot increase the quoted and agreed price. The price can only be varied if the scope of work changes or if contract clauses allow for an increase in price under certain circumstances. Clients prefer lump sum contracts for a simple reason – the full costs are known before the actual project starts and the price is guaranteed not to exceed the agreed amount. It is also much easier to budget and to stay within those budgetary limits.

Consultants don't particularly like this type of flat fee, especially in cases where the work isn't clearly defined, so they tend to use a conservative approach in calculating their costs. An extra ten or fifteen per cent contingency is usually built in to cover unexpected costs. One of the advantages of this method is that it forces discipline and encourages consultants to move outside their comfort zones and look for new, better and more cost-effective ways of achieving the objectives of the contract. In such a process, new competitive solutions are sought and the old, traditional views and processes are challenged.

❏ *Schedule of fees*. The consultant is paid according to the agreed schedule of rates, usually on an hourly or daily basis. The flat hourly or daily rate a consultant charges includes all his expenses, such as office expenditure, travel, telephone etc.

❏ *Fully reimbursable*. The consultant is reimbursed according to the agreed schedule of rates, plus other expenses that he incurs during the course of the project. Both schedule of fees and fully reimbursable contracts are made on a 'best effort' basis. The consultant's brief or offer is basically his estimate of the time and material needed to do the job. He does not, however, guarantee either that the work will be finished in the estimated time or that the initial assumptions, projections and methods are correct. This invariably leaves clients open to additional charges.

❏ *Retainer*. Retaining arrangements are those where consultants are likely to be called upon frequently to perform certain services on a regular basis. The consultant guarantees his availability whenever required, for an agreed number of hours or days, which are covered by the retainer fee, usually paid monthly. Additional time spent on a project is billed as the hours are incurred. In some arrangements the unused time each month is forfeit and the next month starts afresh. Some consultants agree to the accumulation of the unused time as a credit until the end of the calendar or financial year, when the record is wiped clean and the arrangement is renewed, renegotiated or terminated.

Some consultants use retainers as a way of determining if a client has the funds to retain them and the willingness to enter into such an arrangement. When a consultant starts work without a retainer, he extends his trust by crediting the client, having no guarantee that he'll be paid later.

Smart move
Although some consultants do charge excessive fees, many have quite acceptable fee scales. To get a feeling about their overheads and profits, spare a few minutes and calculate your own hourly rate. Identify all costs your employer must cover in order to keep you employed, including your salary and benefits. You will be surprised how quickly the figure goes up. When you consider consultants' expenses and the income the specialists merit, most fees are understandable.

Costs – the difference between control and monitoring

A very common oversight many clients make is substituting monitoring for control. This especially applies to cost control. In many cases what actually gets done is cost monitoring and recording, where costs are simply recorded and reported as they occur, resulting in a higher cost forecast at the end of each period. Cost control is what really keeps the cost from escalating and projects under budget. The difference is enormous: one is an active, forward-orientated approach, a set or sequence of actions taken to ensure that a project is finished on time, at minimum costs while meeting the required specifications; the other is just a passive overview and data-gathering exercise.

Costs should be controlled by both clients and consultants. In the case of a fixed-price contract that usually is the case. When assignments based on hourly rates are considered, consultants generally aren't too keen on minimising the costs, because an expense to a client is usually an income to a consultant.

Some consultants tend to charge more at the beginning of a project, rather than distributing the billings evenly through the life of a project. This means that the amount of work done is less than the charge billed to a client for that period. The reason for that practice is twofold. It improves the consulting firm's cash flow and makes the client think that the consultants are working harder on the study than they really are. Although the practice doesn't pose a serious threat to your pockets (it doesn't mean that you'll be overbilled at the end of the project), beware of consultants who use this guerrilla tactic.

Smart Move
Are you generally too busy to monitor consultants and their progress? Find the time! Create the time! Today's assignment is, if not more, at least equally as important as tomorrow's contract.

The question isn't whether a client should monitor and control project costs, but how those costs are to be monitored and controlled, and when. To answer these questions, we'll arbitrarily group the 'compressible' project costs (those that can be minimised or reduced) into three general groups: prevention and contingency planning costs; monitoring and controlling costs; and failure costs. The importance and the effect prevention and contingency planning has on the total project cost is illustrated in Fig. 3.7 below. Here we see that by a relatively small increase in prevention planning and control, the monitoring and controlling costs are slightly reduced, but the costs occurring as a consequence of failures, delays and errors during the life of a project are drastically reduced.

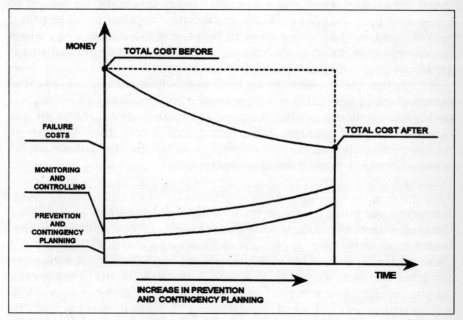

FIG. 3.7

Alternative methods of payment

In this age of tight budgets, strictly controlled cash flows and cost-reducing efforts, a growing number of clients are looking for alternative methods of payment for consulting fees. Parting with hard cash is always difficult and less painful ways of remuneration are being sought. One of these ways is bartering. Another is some sort of profit-sharing arrangement.

Also called 'venture marketing', the latter method simply means that the client agrees to compensate the consultant not through a standard set fee, but entirely on a percentage basis; a percentage of the improvement that will result as a consequence of the consultant's work. This improvement is usually expressed as a percentage increase in sales, but can also be a decrease in costs, lower absenteeism, increased productivity, or some other measurable parameter of the client's business. Some consulting firms like these ventures, for they provide them with shrewd investment vehicles and leveraging tools for their management know-how. Some consultants even buy the companies they formerly advised or are currently consulting.

Although the advantage this arrangement brings to the client is obvious (not having to invest any cash and being able to afford consulting services despite the current financial position), there are also many drawbacks. First and foremost, consultants must be willing to invest their time and effort without immediate compensation. The payoff period could be long. They have to be willing to take the risk, which means that they must truly believe in the client's venture and in the growth or improvement potential.

For clients, the problem is of both a psychological and a financial nature. If the project turns out to be successful, the client will not be able to determine whether that success eventuated as a result of the consultant's efforts or some other factor. In any case, they will have to pay a significant percentage of that windfall to the consultant. A textbook recipe for bitterness and resentment.

Bartering – a good business or an unhealthy practice?

For some clients bartering is something that should be avoided. They feel it isn't legal or binding. It projects an image of a client who cannot pay cash and is desperate. One side always feels hard done by. It seems that the other side benefits much more than yourself. It's hard to put a value on the services you are receiving, while the cost of your services or products is generally known. And it always feels as if someone is doing you a favour, for which you should feel obliged and indebted.

So bartering may not always be the best option, but it could be a sensible one in some cases. This is why:

- ❑ It can turn a difficult or less likely sale into an easy and profitable one
- ❑ If negotiated smartly, it saves you money
- ❑ It creates bonds between clients and consultants
- ❑ It keeps your production lines busy and your chequebook intact

Say yours is a computer company that imports, installs and supports local network products, including software. You need an auditor to check your books before you lodge a tax return. You have a strong working relationship with a management consulting company which has accounting specialists and provides that type of service. They want to integrate their office PCs into a network, so they can share software, printers and backup facilities, send internal mail via the network and improve communication and data exchange.

Bingo. They do your books for a few years, you give them a network and maintain it. They have found a profitable contract for a couple of weeks per year which might not otherwise have been billable time. You have sold software and hardware which might not have been bought otherwise. They would have had to raise a request for capital expenditure, and, if approved, wait until the next financial year. Then they would have gone for tender, and you might have lost. This way, you flog off cheap Taiwanese fiddly bits, get a superb auditing job done and keep the Big Taxation Brother happy. *Voilà!*

Variations – a 'headache' word
Before going into detailed project analysis and before you brief a consultant, decide on two basic categories of features – 'must have' and 'nice to have'. This will help you not only in communicating your goals and requirements to the consultant, but also in deciding what to leave out should you run into monetary problems due to budget restrictions or should the project run late.

Variations are usually caused by these two events or by the change of scope of consulting services. They may be expressed in written or oral form. A written contract may be varied by a subsequent verbal agreement and a verbal contract can just as well be varied by a written amendment.

Don't hesitate to talk about money
Talking about money, and particularly about negotiating consulting fees, is one of the most uncomfortable tasks in dealing with consultants. As a consequence, clients generally avoid it in their face-to-face meetings with consultants and, in the end, pay for it dearly.

Fees should be discussed as early in the process as possible, and you, the client, should be the one to initiate the discussion, because consultants seldom will. They may prefer to fax or mail to you their standard 'Schedule of Fees'. By all means let them do that. Then start negotiating and see how you can bring those rates down. Shying away from discussions about money is a very unhealthy habit from your accountant's point of view.

The first stage in any contact between a client and a consultant is always the mutual evaluation of profitability. Both sides are looking for clues and indicators that will help them predict the benefits of the endeavour. Those benefits aren't necessarily of monetary value, although one may argue that every benefit may somehow be linked to profits.

Since potential benefits are hard to predict accurately at this early stage, it may be a wise policy to try to get as many concessions as possible from the consultant. Discounts are always the bottom line of these early negotiating efforts.

Why would consultants give you a discount on their standard rates? The reasons abound. If you are a new and reputable client, they may want to add your organisation to their customer list. Some may find your project interesting or are, for some reason, personally attached or attracted to it. They may see it as an opportunity for learning and broadening their expertise in that area or an opportunity for getting more projects in the future, should they do a good job and satisfy the client. Firms and individuals starting out desperately want to build their practice and are usually keen to get the job, even at reduced profits. Large or long-term projects, even at significantly reduced rates, are viewed as a steady and planned source of income, compared with the erratic and unpredictable workload brought in by smaller, occasional jobs.

Expenses are a significant yet often neglected contributor to overall project cost. In most cases, expenses are reimbursable, with the additional mark-up fee of some 10 to 15 per cent. Some are easily understood and controllable, such as travel expenses, which can be identified, estimated and budgeted for. Others are difficult to predict and even more difficult to control. These are for example secetarial and other administrative costs (printing, copying, plotting, binding, courier, telephone, fax, drafting, computer usage, etc.).

This can be dealt with in two ways. One option is to keep a close eye on these expenses by requesting an itemised log with all relevant bills charged to the project and questioning anything that seems odd or higher than normal. The other way of minimising administrative costs is to provide as many of them as is physically and logistically possible in-house, by making facilities available to consultants or having your staff do the work for them. This is usually a much cheaper option.

PROJECT CHECKLIST

Project definition
- ☐ Issue or problem raised/flagged
- ☐ Initial investigation
- ☐ Project file created
- ☐ Consultation
- ☐ Analysis of options

- ❑ Initial plan
- ❑ Preliminary definition report
- ❑ Review
- ❑ Approval to proceed

Detailed investigation
- ❑ Detailed analysis
- ❑ Detailed definition report
- ❑ Proposed methodology (in-house or consultant?)
- ❑ Review
- ❑ Approval to proceed
- ❑ Develop budget-secure financing
- ❑ Consultant's brief

Contract management
- ❑ Initial discussions with consultants
- ❑ Formal issue of the brief
- ❑ Request for fee proposals
- ❑ Evaluate fee proposals
- ❑ Discussions/presentations
- ❑ Award of the contract
- ❑ Contract letter

Project execution phase
- ❑ Start-up meeting
- ❑ Project execution plan
- ❑ Monitor progress
- ❑ Information/data gathering
- ❑ Problem analysis
- ❑ Proposed solution

Implementation phase
- ❑ Implementation tasks
- ❑ Meetings
- ❑ Variations and additions

Evaluation and termination phase
- ❑ Evaluation of results and achievements
- ❑ Final report/study
- ❑ Communicate findings to all involved or affected
- ❑ Declare project closed

Chapter 4: Monitoring and controlling consultants

Why some consultants don't do what they're supposed to do and what can be done about it

> *All my life, I've known better than to depend on the experts. How could I have been so stupid as to let them go ahead?*
>
> John F. Kennedy on the Bay of Pigs disaster

Managing people, assets, projects or organisations is a tough job. Management is not an exact quantitative discipline such as science or engineering, despite business schools' preachings and their emphasis on the quantitative aspects of management. They don't deal with the qualitative aspect of the profession because they don't know how to. There are no management approaches, techniques or methods that are universally accepted, applicable or appropriate.

Engineers, accountants and other technically orientated, quantitative people generally feel that things are more predictable and much easier to control than people. This isn't necessarily so. Everyone who understands people realises that they are predictable, too. And everything that is predictable is controllable. Consultants are not an exception to that rule.

A cookbook approach

Management, and especially managing projects and consultants, is basically nothing more than a collection of successful recipes. Each 'cook' has his own secrets; he maintains and regularly updates and improves his recipes, the ones that work for him and produce the desired results.

There is no universal solution to the management problem. It isn't in the latest fads. It isn't in the consultants. It isn't in truisms. Everybody is still searching.

The emphasis on the latest ideas is obvious amongst both clients and consultants. The gullibility factor makes consultants open their arms and embrace new fads indiscriminately, develop a whole range of marketable services around them and flog them off to even more gullible consumers, who eagerly clutch at every straw offered by consultants.

Clients seldom realise that, when it comes to choosing the most appropriate management technique for solving their particular business problems, some advisers and consultants simply cannot be relied on, for one basic reason. Having vested interests in certain methods and solutions they are promoting, in many cases they won't admit their infallibility. They emphasise successes and keep quiet about failures. Since many consultants promote their own products, methods and solutions, critical evaluation of their motives, biases and interest spheres is mandatory.

Every company wants to make a superior product, build a motivated and competent workforce, empower them, keep its customers happy, make the best use of its resources, respond quickly to changes in the market and position itself strongly against the competitors. The aims are universal and easy to define. The means for achieving those aims are various and not universally applicable. The critical question now is not 'What?' but 'How?'

Tainted image

One of the reasons for the tainted image of the consulting profession and current cynicism in the ranks of business managers and other users of consulting services is a credibility gap. What is promised is quite often different from what is delivered. 'Blue skying' methods used in securing a contract are the major contributors to this illusion.

The keys to competent and professional consulting are the consultant's ability to recognise his own limits, integrity and the willingness to keep operating within those limits. You, the client, also have to recognise his limitations and keep them firmly embedded in your mind. Your ignorance is strength, but only for the consultants. For you, it spells trouble.

Every client gets the consultant he deserves. If you allow a consultant to get away with high fees, poor performance or assignments that are too long, without a clear objective and which result in no real benefit to you, there is no one to blame but yourself.

Methods of control

The importance of constant control

> Forecast: To observe that which has passed, and guess it will happen again.
>
> Frank McKinney Hubbard

In the managing process, alternatives, options and directions should constantly be evaluated, analysed, planned and followed. The constant feedback on the course you are taking, your aims and the speed at which you are achieving them will minimise sidetracking and help you reach your goals in the shortest possible time. In addition to the feedback process, which is corrective in nature (you act upon things that are already happening), there is feed forward, which is a pro-active process (you anticipate events and act in advance in order to prevent things from happening or to change the course developments may take).

The concept of critical path is another very useful tool in this process. A critical path is the shortest, the most efficient, or the most appropriate course of interrelated actions and steps to take towards achieving a target. There is always some room for error in the critical path. Finding your critical path will help you to move towards your goal even when you get sidetracked or things don't go the way they were planned.

Be ready for the future. Anticipate and predict. See possiblities before

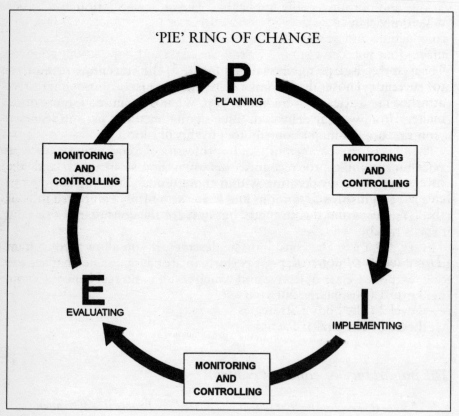

'PIE' RING OF CHANGE

P
PLANNING

MONITORING
AND
CONTROLLING

MONITORING
AND
CONTROLLING

E
EVALUATING

I
IMPLEMENTING

MONITORING
AND
CONTROLLING

FIG 4.1

they become obvious. Only by doing this will you be able to surpass your competition.

Both as a starting point in your analysis, and as a permanent self-analysis tool, some questions should constantly be asked along the way:

- ❑ What are my alternatives?
- ❑ What are the pros and cons of each alternative?
- ❑ What developments could affect my mission?
- ❑ What knowledge and skills will I need to successfully complete my mission?
- ❑ Where and how do I acquire the knowledge and develop the skills needed?
- ❑ How will my choices affect my future?
- ❑ What are the critical factors of my success?
- ❑ How do I control those critical factors?

Before you make a decision or a choice of importance, you first have to conclude and appreciate the fact that a choice or decision has to be made; that you can't simply ignore the issue and hope it will go away. The next step is to recognise various demands that have to be met for you to succeed. Those demands and the assessment of potential risks attached to various options will have an impact on the final decision you make. This is a typical decision-making pattern. Follow it and watch your decision-making skills and habits improve significantly.

Don't assume anything and don't take anything for granted. Keep your finger on the project pulse and keep asking questions. The rule of inversely proportional control could be summarised as: The less interest, care and control you take, the longer the consultants will take to finish the assignment and the more expensive the whole project will be.

Three levels of control

Level 1 (The base): Objectives
Level 2 (The body): Strategies
Level 3 (The peak): Tactics

FIG. 4.2

Many inexperienced clients don't quite understand the difference between objectives, strategies and tactics. An objective is your goal. It is simply what you want to achieve. A strategy is the way you plan to achieve your objective, a general approach to the problem. Your strategy in turn dictates your tactics, which are more detailed ways of getting what you want.

Cornerstones of control

> *Ready? Shoot! Aim!*
>   Japanese view of Western management techniques

THE FOUR CORNERSTONES OF EFFECTIVE CONTROL

Clarity
Conducive environment
Commitment
Consistency

FIG. 4.3

❑ *The first cornerstone is clarity.* Simply stated, it isn't enough for a client to know what is needed. Those thoughts, instructions, goals and ideas have to be communicated clearly and effectively to the consultant, so he knows exactly what the client is talking about.

❑ *The second cornerstone is conducive environment.* A positive and supportive atmosphere which will be conducive to problem-solving and change-implementation is the soil in which the seeds that will bear the fruit of the consultant's labour will be sown. Your task as a client is to provide that fertile soil. Treat consultants as partners, rather than adversaries. Make sure they have the tools, information and support they need, and help them when they find themselves in trouble.

There are two aspects of the environment which have an impact on consulting projects: the client's company culture itself, and the suitability and compatibility between that environment and the consultant: his personality, goals, ambitions, values, way of thinking, communicating and operating. Many problems and disputes emerge as a result of incompatibility or conflict between the client's organisation and the consultant. We may call it a poor fit. Some clients blame themselves or the consultants for poor performance and project failure, while the real cause of the problem is simply the wrong corporate environment and a lack of support.

❑ *The third cornerstone is commitment.* Just as you supervise and manage your own employees, with a commitment to producing results by keeping constant control over their projects, work methods, practices and hours worked, you should be equally committed to keeping firm and constant control of consulting projects.

❑ *The fourth cornerstone is consistency.* Effective control is continuous and consistent. It follows the predetermined path set by policies, guidelines and effective monitoring and controlling practices, and it leads towards the ultimate goal of minimising costs, avoiding problems and maximising the benefits of each consulting project.

Consistency is mostly achieved through the use of project management procedures which should be tailored to suit your particular organisation and the business you are in. These procedures not only prescribe the sequence of steps you have to take in managing consultants, but also explain the reasons for each activity and the benefits that will follow the proper implementation of each step. In some cases, where possible and desirable, the procedures also specify how certain tasks, both clients' and consultants', are to be done. This obviously isn't possible in some less structured and less defined consulting assignments, such as research and development or management projects, and may not be desirable from the viewpoint of creativity, innovation or flexibility.

Consistency through the use of project management procedures is achieved due to the fact that no matter who the responsible person is in the client's organisation and who the consultant is, the methodology used, the accompanying files and documentation created and all aspects of the project are easily understood by others (if a change of personnel occurs or a follow-up project goes ahead) and can be integrated with other projects a client may work on. Simple control and monitoring methods, introduced from the start of a project, are far more effective than complex methods introduced when it's too late.

The concept of feedback

One of the fundamental problems in the use of consultants is lack of feedback. The universal notion among modern managers is that consultants take care of the theory and its practical application. In this equation there is no room for feedback. The consultant's work is assumed to be right and the management is focused on the task of making it work in practice.

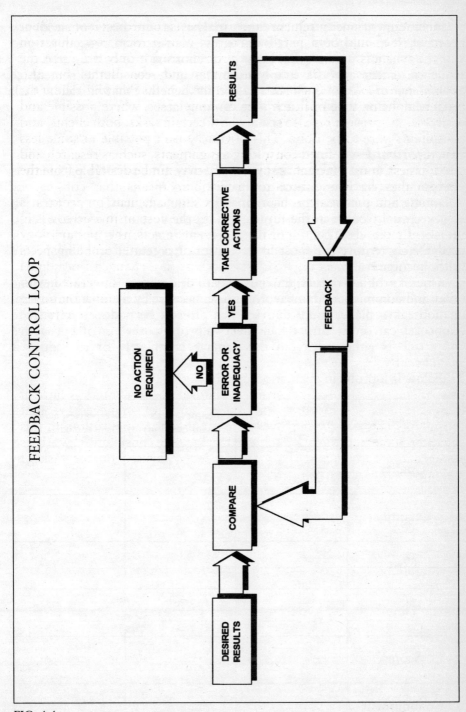

FEEDBACK CONTROL LOOP

DESIRED RESULTS

COMPARE

ERROR OR INADEQUACY

NO — NO ACTION REQUIRED

YES

TAKE CORRECTIVE ACTIONS

RESULTS

FEEDBACK

FIG. 4.4

Achievement measurement and analysis is the basis of feedback control. It should be a part of progress management procedures and serve as the missing link that turns cost reporting into cost control.

Achievement analysis simply estimates and records the percentage completed of each major task and predicts whether that particular task will be done on time or if it will be running late.

Feed forward

The easiest, most efficient and most effective time to solve problems is before they have a chance to occur. This means that contingency planning and potential problem analysis should be used as preparation for eventual trouble in the future. This is the core of proactive or feed forward methods. The aim of these preventive actions is to partially or completely remove the most likely causes of potential problems before they become real ones.

Once a problem occurs, the only way to deal with it is to react in some way and minimise the damage. Minimise, because by the time the control action takes place, some damage has already been done. A reactive approach can only reduce the impact of a problem; the aim of a proactive approach is either to avoid the damage completely or to reduce it significantly.

Below is a problem evaluation matrix:

	What could go wrong, how and why?	Indicators, signs and manifestations	Responses, actions, remedies
Quality			
Quantity			
Cost			
Time			
Scope			
Commitment			

There are four aspects of preventative control:

❑ Recognition of weaknesses, inconsistencies, vulnerabilities
❑ Identification of potential problems
❑ Investigation of the likely causes of those problems
❑ Implementation of preventative and contingent actions

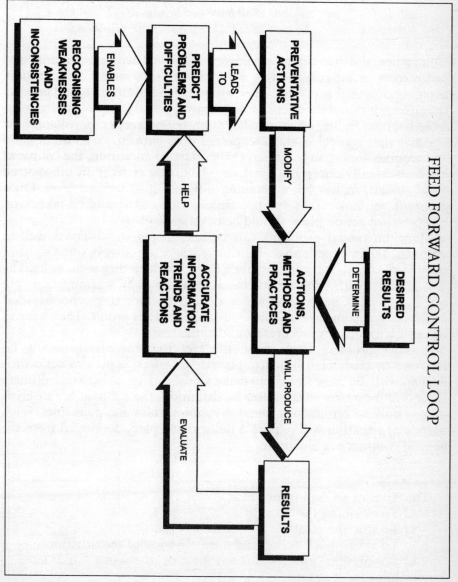

FIG. 4.5

When things start to go wrong

'Would you tell me,' said Alice, a little timidly, 'why you are painting those roses?'
Five and Seven said nothing, but looked at Two. Two began in a low voice, 'Why, the fact is, you see, Miss, this here ought to have been a red rose-tree, and we put a white one in by mistake; and if the Queen was to find it out, we should all have our heads cut off, you know.'
Lewis Carroll *Alice's Adventures in Wonderland*

Companies and individual employees who deal with consultants and contractors invest considerable amounts of time, money and effort in avoiding potential problems, preventing misunderstandings and keeping resources, time and materials under control.

As happens in life, no matter how tightly one keeps control and how effective that control is, the unexpected does happen, crises do develop and trouble does emerge. When things start to go wrong, the course of events is usually uncertain. That very fact, that crisis is an unexpected development, makes crisis planning difficult at a detailed level. On a general level, however, some precautions can and should be taken and blueprints of action plans should be developed.

Many unwanted problems can be anticipated or observed well in advance. To an experienced client's eye, there are always some signs of trouble ahead, no matter how subtle or well hidden they seem to be. The first concern with problem-solving is that the early warning signs are often ignored. Clients simply don't want to face them, hoping that problems will somehow magically disappear. They won't. They have to be dealt with quickly, accurately and consistently.

Another problem stems from the fact that there is generally no recovery or crisis plan in place. Having an effective plan of action for dealing with the unexpected can make all the difference between ultimate success and catastrophic failure. By definition, the contingency or crisis plan is only an outline of general principles, rules and guidelines. Each particular situation will require a tailor-made plan, developed from the general contingency blueprint.

The Aims of a Contingency Plan
- ❏ To minimise the damage
- ❏ To stop the escalating sequence of events
- ❏ To allow quick action and normalisation of the situation
- ❏ To prevent unwanted situations of the same kind from happening again

The psychology of a crisis

Clients and consultants react to problems and crises in standard, predictable ways. These are the most common responses:

❑ *Disillusionment and disbelief.* Disbelief is usually the first reaction when problems strike. 'This can't be true, I checked it twice!' 'Why does this always happen to me?' and 'How is this possible?' are the most common exclamations.

The ostrich effect, when clients bury their heads in the sand, is a typical manifestation of disbelief. They refuse to acknowledge the situation and freeze; do nothing, say nothing, as if the problem doesn't exist. By the time they regain their composure and self-control, the problem has usually escalated further, the available rememdies are fewer and more difficult to apply and the potential damage is greater. The lesson: Don't wait until it's too late. Act quickly, swiftly and energetically.

❑ *Panic.* A very common response, although a totally counterproductive and undesirable one. Minds work at full speed, vision is clouded, adrenalin boils, emotions run high, ulcers become active. It is helped by certain traits of the individual's personality, such as lack of composure, experience and organised thinking, and also by external organisational factors: lack of contingency plans, support from one's peers and superiors or effective communication.

❑ *Straw-grabbing.* Desperate clinging to straws or blindly accepting the first option that comes along, promising quick-fix solutions and immediate relief. Solutions of this kind in many cases work against the client, triggering new problems further down the line.

❑ *Bouncing blame.* The search for scapegoats begins almost immediately after a problem appears. This is the law of human nature. People blame everybody but themselves. Clients blame consultants, consultants blame clients, clouding the main issues, stirring emotions and hurting feelings.

❑ *Hurt feelings.* Every problem, dispute or crisis damages the relationship between client and consultant. It provokes ill-feeling and costs money. How much, it's impossible to estimate. What price do you attach to a productive, professional and mutually beneficial relationship? When everything is going smoothly, there are things clients and consultants never talk about. These are the issues they have total control over and the power to change – their own actions, behaviour and performance. Only in crises does this communication take place.

❏ *Litigation.* When you decide to go and see your lawyer, wanting to fight the dispute to the bitter end, you not only help him become rich, but you also embark on a violent, traumatic, time- and money-consuming path. Many clients don't even consider the possibility of incurring high legal costs, let alone think about other implications, such as lost time or emotional trauma.

Contract law is extremely complicated and time-consuming. It involves highly specialised (and therefore expensive) lawyers, who have to go through a myriad previous cases to decide which ones are applicable and to frame the strategy accordingly. There are many grey areas and conflicting judgments.

There are more effective and cheaper alternatives to litigation. The most powerful one is called communication. Any dispute can be resolved if only parties are willing to communicate. Once the commitment to alternative dispute resolution is made and the dialogue starts, finding a workable solution and a suitable compromise is just a matter of time.

There is an ounce of good in every truckload of bad

> How many a dispute could have been deflated into a single paragraph if the disputants had dared to define their terms.
>
> Aristotle

Every problem encountered, every crisis dealt with and every dispute between a client and a consultant is, above all, an excellent opportunity to learn about ourselves, about the systems within which we operate and about others. This valuable experience cannot be gained by reading books or attending courses. It is only in real life that we learn the lessons which should help us not to make the same mistakes again.

Another positive effect of an otherwise negative situation is the opportunity to change individual and organisational prejudices, fallacies, biases, preconceived notions and outdated perceptions. Much-needed changes in ways of working, thinking and operating can be accelerated, allowing fresh thinking and new views to emerge. Basically, every mistake made and every difficulty faced should be used to improve yourself professionally and personally. Chances often come disguised as crisis, misfortune or temporary defeat. The Chinese symbol for crisis is made up of two strokes of the pen. One stands for danger, the other for opportunity.

Why projects go over budget
There are two reasons why projects go over budget. One is the project

manager's and consultant's inability to keep costs down. The other is hidden in the very core of the budgeting and tendering game. Both clients and consultants benefit from underestimating the costs from the beginning.

Consultants know that if they estimate project costs realistically, with an essential inbuilt contingency, and if they quote corresponding fees, their chances of winning the assignment will be greatly reduced, because they'll be undercut by their competitors.

Clients, on the other hand, in order to get their projects approved by upper management or boards of directors, usually underestimate costs and overestimate the benefits expected as a result, so their 'cost benefit analysis' keeps the accountants and everybody else happy and preserves that cosy feeling of progress.

Dealing with problems
There are three ways an individual or an organisation may deal with a problem.

- ❑ Predict it
- ❑ Ignore it
- ❑ Respond to it

All three work in real life. Only the last one produces results.

Smart Move
Practise preventative medicine. Watch for early signs of trouble or difficulty. Use cheap aspirins. Don't allow the situation to deteriorate to the point where major (and expensive) surgery is required.

Disputes
Every client–consultant relationship resembles a marriage. Both parties agreed to it and entered into the relationship of their own free will. They also brought in their expectations, feelings, hopes, ideas and concerns. Many client–consultant relationships end up the same way as increasing numbers of marriages do – in disputes, with hurt feelings, broken illusions and shattered dreams. What would you say is the main reason for such an appalling rate of divorce in our society? It is lack of communication. If lack of communication can break a marriage, can you imagine what it can do to a less binding and less stable consulting relationship?

Taking corrective action

Fairy Godmother, where were you when I needed you?
Charles Perrault, *Cinderella*

Duing the progression of a project, there will be times when actual will not correspond to planned. The reasons can vary from unrealistic planning, lack of resources or delays in delivery of goods, through to unexpected problems or changes of scope in midstream.

These situations require corrective action at a proper moment. Taking action too early is not always beneficial in the long run. Some of the inadequacies are self-correcting. A smooth and steady progress belongs to textbooks. In real life, at any point in time, you are either behind or in front. What separates a good plan from the rest is the fact that those leads and lags will (ideally) cancel each other out, leaving you in front or finishing as per your schedule.

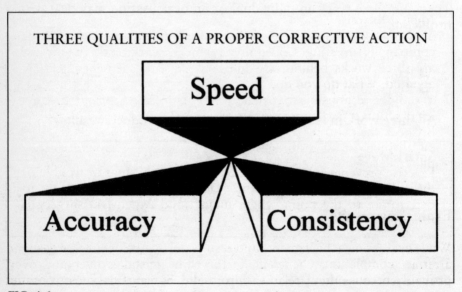

THREE QUALITIES OF A PROPER CORRECTIVE ACTION

Speed

Accuracy

Consistency

FIG. 4.6

There are a couple of options for getting a job back on schedule. The remaining work can be re-examined and the lost time may be recovered by shortening the phases and tasks that follow. This option usually compromises on quality, but doesn't increase the costs. The other option is to deploy more resources. This increases cost, but normally brings a project back on track. Unfortunately, there are no guarantees that more people on a project will mean that the progress will be speeded up. The extra costs associated with coordination of additional workers, such as organising them and helping them get up to speed, can outweigh the benefits the additional staff bring to the project. This basically means that it is possible that more people will actually do less work at additional cost.

When you are less than happy about something a consultant has done poorly or hasn't done at all, there are two steps that have to be taken. Firstly, express your dissatisfaction openly and explicitly. Secondly, ask for a remedy. Just complaining or stating a grievance isn't enough. You have to ask for an issue to be resolved and the situation to be rectified.

By asking for an immediate remedy, you avoid the risk of a consultant questioning the legitimacy of your complaint, and force him to focus on the corrective action. By taking the initiative in your hands, you make his life easier too, because he doesn't have to guess how you feel about the whole issue. Most importantly, the corrective action is more likely to be based on your interests rather than on theirs.

Mental Exercise
You are in charge of electrical design for a new plant in which your company is investing. Consulting engineers working on the project are three weeks behind schedule and top management is clearly agitated. What do you do?
a) Call the responsible manager in the engineering firm and threaten legal action if they don't deliver the designs on time?
b)Check the contract to ascertain their liability?
c)Call them in for an urgent meeting and agree on a contingency plan to bring the project back on schedule?

Evaluating results

While evaluating achievements and results during the life of a project and after its completion, clients make the same mistakes over and over, probably because they are so easy to make. Some of the most common ones are also very easy to avoid.

Whilst estimating the percentage of the project that is completed, don't assume that the work done corresponds to the time that has elapsed since the beginning of the project or to the amount of funds spent to date. If a task is estimated to require a hundred man-hours, the fact that a consultant has spent fifty hours on it doesn't necessarily mean that it is fifty per cent complete.

Don't always expect a consultant's study to confirm your own ideas. Preconceived expectations are one thing; reality is usually something quite different.

Don't judge results by the size of the report. What should be evaluated is how closely the results match your brief or scope of work. If everything that was specified to be done has been done, the fact that some irrelevant details are missing from the report is a sign that a consultant knows how to distil information and values your time by presenting only relevant matter. There is no worse insult to a client's intelligence than submitting a pumped-up report where the same information is presented over and over, in the introduction, in the body of the report and then in the conclusion (which is almost as long as the body).

The best indicator of project success is the feeling that the client and consultant together have achieved their objective of either solving a problem or improving a certain aspect of the client's company, which has become a better business than it was before the project began.

Guerrilla school for shrewd clients

Beware of 'one-off' assignments

The trouble with most employers is that they don't hire consultants often enough. They are not sure how consultants operate, how to deal with them or what to expect from them. More often than not, clients don't know how to communicate their requirements and they certainly don't realise when they are being taken for a ride.

But the problem reflects on consultants as well. They know they were hired on an *ad hoc* basis and that another assignment with the same employer isn't very likely. Left with no real possibility of future work, their only motive for doing a good job, apart from their own ethics and professionalism, is the fear of the powerful, negative, 'word of mouth' publicity.

Relying on someone's ethics and professionalism is a desperate and certainly not very wise business move. To protect yourself from being ambushed, you had better adopt the following guerrilla tactics.

Invest in long-term relationships

A regular customer is worth between six and twelve potential customers. That's why no consultant will risk damaging an established relationship based on loyalty and trust, by doing a sloppy job, charging too much, being inflexible, narrow-minded or simply unwilling to accommodate a regular client's wishes.

This is a very important fact. It tips the scales of power in the client's favour and gives them a leverage in a negotiating process when clinching a deal. Don't be afraid to exercise that power, your clients probably do the same to you. Sometimes you give, sometimes you take. In this instance take as much as you can without humiliating the other side or making it impossible for them not to lose money.

Keep the assignments short

The consulting knife, no matter how sharp and effective it may be at the beginning of a job, invariably loses its edge as the project goes on. There are two significant problems with marathon engagements. After a while, a consultant, being a human being, starts to feel complacent and to become an insider. He is less and less of an objective, unbiased outsider and more and more of a domesticated employee, losing his fresh views and getting used to 'the way we do things around here' type of conditioning. Many clients start treating him like a permanent employee, forgetting the real reason he was hired and the high hourly rate he's charging.

Another, equally dangerous sign is the slower working pace which characterises long assignments, resulting from the lack of time pressure and the constant client control. It is a fact of life that consultants work more efficiently and expeditiously during shorter assignments. This doesn't necessarily mean that they will deliberately slow down their activities and adopt a relaxed attitude when working on longer projects, just that they are prone to embrace the slower working pace which may creep up during prolonged engagements.

Protect yourself from getting steamrollered

'I am absolutely sure he never knew what hit him.'
Chief surgeon to the wife of another manager,
a casualty of his own incautiousness

❑ *Make sure all documents and materials are returned*. During the course of an assignment, consultants borrow internal documents, drawings and equipment from clients. Before the work starts, specify in the contract that all borrowed items of any kind have to be returned upon the completion of the assignment. Then, when that time comes, follow the issue up and make sure they are returned, and in mint condition, too.

❑ *Don't fall in love with a name*. It isn't uncommon for large, relatively diversified consulting firms to be awarded contracts simply because of their well-known name, despite the obvious lack of experience or expertise in that particular area.

To make general assumptions about what a particular firm is capable of doing has always been and always will be a very difficult task for clients. Assumptions make poor foundations on which to base a decision and many clients pay a high price for assuming that bigger is better, without checking what specific experience (if any) the firm in question may or may not have.

❑ *Never give an important project to an untried consultant, no matter how good their reputation is.* If you like the firm or the individual, give them a trial or a pilot project. Should you discover that you can work together, move on to more ambitious and significant projects. Do it gradually. As the cost of everything has gone up, so has the cost of failure.

❑ *Keep constant, firm, no-nonsense control. Never give up.*

Squeezing the lemons dry
❑ *Being available, but not too available.* Building illusions of power is the fastest way towards being perceived as strong and influential by your peers and consultants alike. One of the methods used in image-building is 'the busy body syndrome'. In other words, the more difficult you make it for a consultant to see you, the more important you are going to seem! When facing important people, consultants, just like anybody else, become intimidated, nervous and less demanding. Intimidated, nervous or less demanding consultants are much easier to deal with than composed, self-assured and demanding ones. Remember that a consultant held at arm's length will unconsciously try to come under the client's control.

❑ *Playing the qualifying game.* People want what they can't have or what is difficult to get. This is the psychological base for playing the qualifying game. A client, from the very first contact with a consultant, establishes the ground by planting obstacles in the consultant's path towards winning the assignment.

Constantly and explicitly, consultants are reminded that the project requires special knowledge and expertise, detailed proposals and capability statements, qualifying exercises (during which a client picks their brains for free) and other requirements. This is followed by an encouraging statement that there is a chance they can win the contract. This makes consultants relieved and encouraged, only to be subjected to further 'qualifying' pressure.

❑ *Using a 'principal' plot.* Even if you haven't got a principal and have the power to make a decision or a commitment on the spot – don't rush. Invent a principal. Make it more difficult for them, make them work harder at trying to make you act as a mediator, because that's exactly how you should try to position yourself. Appear to be sympathetic, but quickly point out the difficulties that lie ahead, unless . . . Unless, of course, they change some unfavourable terms in your favour!

Let them wait a couple of days until you speak to your boss, legal department, accounting department and other intimidating 'obstacles' in the consultant's mind. In those couple of days, the balance of power will swing significantly in your favour and an otherwise tough stand on the part of the consultant will be softened up.

❑ *Practising downgrading tactics.* Downgrading is the simplest and most effective method of dealing with unrealistic demands or inflated consultants' perceptions of their own importance and value. Getting a good deal from a consultant who has an inflated opinion of himself and who feels empowered in the client-consultant relationship is almost impossible. Downgrading puts them in the position where they have to prove themselves to you. This is particularly useful during the initial stages of briefing consultants and negotiating terms, when they tend to brag about their accomplishments and exaggerate their ability. Downgrading sends a clear message that you are not interested in blue-skying and that the only thing you care about is their performance on *your* job!

❑ *Making sudden requests.* Many consultants have great difficulty saying a very simple single-syllable word – *no*. This is particularly true in situations when they are faced with a sudden and unexpected request from a client and they have to make a decision on the spot. They may feel further obligated not to refuse the client for fear of losing future contracts or damaging the long-term relationship. Clients, it goes without saying, benefit from this technique more than from any other intimidation tactic.

It isn't necessary to request significant concessions. On the contrary, the tactic works better when used to elicit relatively minor ones. By making constant small gains, which seem insignificant and non-threatening to the consultant, the whole relationship comes under the client's control in no time.

Ask questions

I keep six honest serving men
They taught me all I knew:
Their names are What and Why and When
and How and Where and Who.

Rudyard Kipling

Smart Questions
- ❑ Why do we do it this way?
- ❑ Does it make sense?
- ❑ Why should we change this?
- ❑ Why shouldn't we change this?
- ❑ Are there other, better ways of doing this?
- ❑ What are our competitors doing?
- ❑ What is the core problem?
- ❑ Is this a cause or a consequence?
- ❑ Who can help us solve this problem?
- ❑ What are we trying to achieve?
- ❑ How can we make this better, cheaper or in less time?
- ❑ Is this a good idea?
- ❑ What are the alternatives?
- ❑ Is this the right time/place/method?
- ❑ Are we reinventing the wheel? Has this been done before?
- ❑ Where is the opportunity? How do I recognise it and capitalise on it?
- ❑ What resources do I need and how do I control them?
- ❑ Who can make this project work?
- ❑ What decisions have to be made?
- ❑ Who will be affected by those decisions?
- ❑ Where are we now and where are we going?
- ❑ How do we get there?
- ❑ What can go wrong and why?

Never be afraid of asking questions. The consultants you employ will almost always provide you with an answer, because it's their job. Some questions may make you appear uninformed, naive or superficial. Some may indicate to a consultant your lack of trust, concentration or ability to comprehend more complex, abstract or less obvious ideas and solutions. Don't let all this worry you. It is better to appear 'imperfect' and do something about it than to stay ill-informed, ignorant and, ultimately, unsuccessful.

It is rather difficult to produce specific, detailed questions in a book such as this one, which is of a more general nature, dealing mostly with principles and less with details. Regardless of that, every general question can be reformulated to address very specific issues and to ask for very specific answers.

Pick their brains

Free advice is the sweetest advice, say some clients. These people are extremely skilful when it comes to picking consultants' brains without paying them a penny. There are two ways of getting free advice. The first is an informal method. Invite a consultant to your office. This tilts the balance of power all the way in the client's favour, because *he* came to see *you*, you didn't go to see him. Then start by asking usual, general questions. Gradually, start probing deeper, to see how much the consultant knows about the issue you are interested in.

Some consultants will swallow the bait and go to extreme lengths in explaining what they would do to solve your problem. All you have to do is listen. Some more experienced consulting sharks will be suspicious and will limit their answers and statements to a bare minimum, broad and general. They know that the first rule of clinching a deal is to leave clients wanting more.

The formal version of the same method utilises false invitations to make proposals. A few consulting firms are invited to submit their *detailed* proposals, free of charge, of course. You give them a brief explaining the issue and providing as much information as possible, to make their lives easier and the probability of accepting this scheme more likely. Some firms will refuse to work on this basis, because they know that if the job is to be done properly, many hours will have to be spent preparing the proposal. But you just move on and find some other firm which will be desperate enough to dance to your tune.

Here you are, boy, and there's more to come

This is a very common 'carrot theory' plot. Repeat business is good business. Every manager knows that, and so does every consultant. For consultants, the best incentive for providing the best service possible to clients is the possibility of future work, and they will certainly do a good job if there is a hint of ongoing assignments. You, the manager, have to make them believe that. At the very beginning of a project, be open and let your consultant know that

❏ if they perform well *and*
❏ if they finish the assignment on time *and*
❏ if they charge a fair fee for a fair day's work,

your company will have more work for them in the future. Basically, the message is: 'Do this cheaply and there'll be more where this came from.'

***

Keeping them on their toes

A mining and mineral processing company, part of an international conglomerate, hires a sister company, which specialises in consulting engineering, for most of their engineering projects. Although the engineering consultancy is part of the same group and operates under the same name, a significant percentage of jobs, around 20 to 30 per cent, goes to other engineering consultants who specialise in the mining industry.

The client does not want to be dependent on one consultant in case they become complacent and the quality of their work declines, or in case they perceive that the balance of power has shifted in their favour and charge higher fees as a result.

Chapter 5: Communicating for success

Learn how to listen

The fact is that most people are not good listeners. They never listen to anyone for long. They talk mostly about themselves and interrupt others without waiting for them to finish talking. Even if they don't interrupt, they don't pay attention to what others are saying, because they are busy rehearsing what they are going to say next. That is probably even worse than talking too much, for they are neither making a point nor hearing one.

These are all cardinal sins when talking to consultants. You should listen very carefully not only to what they are saying, but how they are saying it. It is not enough simply to hear, you have to listen aggressively. Listening skills are amongst the most valuable possessions you may have.

Once a meeting starts, you must have a clear idea of how much time to spend on each issue, how much time to devote to answering their questions and when to ask the questions you want to ask. Of course, don't be rigid. Just remember the old cliche: 'Time is money'. It's certainly true when consultants are concerned.

Rules for active listening

❑ Do not jump to conclusions before the other side has finished the statement.

❑ Don't interrupt, even if you strongly disagree. Raise your objections after they finish. Listen for main ideas, as well as for details.

❑ Do not discard the information that you don't want to hear or that you don't like.

❑ If the consultant talks slowly, don't let your mind wander around. No daydreaming. Use that time to analyse what's being said, to anticipate, weigh the evidence, mentally run through the points made and listen 'between the lines' for clues.

❑ Don't tune out if the delivery is poor. Concentrate on content, not errors in speech. Fight or avoid distractions.

Briefing consultants

If his understanding fails, have patience with him.

Solomon

A brief doesn't always have to be in written form, although both clients and consultants prefer a formal, written brief. Even if you do use a written document, it is a very prudent practice to brief the consultant in a face-to-face meeting as well. This provides a good opportunity to explain the background of the problem or the issue, to let him know your views and feelings, to get his initial feedback and to clarify any misunderstanding he may have after reading your written brief.

The structure of all successful speeches, presentations and briefings is similar. The key words are reinforcement and emphasis through repetition and summarising. These are the three basic steps towards an effective brief:

❑ *Tell them what you are going to talk about.*
This is called the introduction.

❑ *Tell them what you are there to talk about.*
This is the body of your brief, your presentation.

❑ *Tell them what you just talked about.*
This is called the summary or the conclusion.

There are some messages you have to communicate to consultants at the very beginning of your relationship. Don't expect them to guess your requirements, feelings and opinions. Tell them:

1. What they are expected to accomplish in their assignment. Precisely define the job that has to be done.
2. The standards they are expected to reach.
3. Your expectations and criteria for evaluation. Emphasise that trying is not enough, doing and accomplishing are the only acceptable actions. Agree on goals and provide a positive, specific feedback.

Progress meetings

One ought, every day at least, to hear a little song, read a good poem, see a fine picture, and, if it were possible, to speak a few reasonable words.

Goethe, *Wilhelm Meister's Apprenticeship*, V, 1

Meeting has become a dirty word, almost a synonym for inefficiency, wasting time and money, mind-boggling discussions and debates. However, despite the fact that most meetings produce far fewer results than they theoretically should, the whole idea of a meeting as a productive communication tool still survives and naturally lends itself to management methods of control.

Guerrilla Tactics for Effective Progress Meetings
❑ *Don't allow people to sit down.* Keep them standing up. That way there is no danger of half of them dozing off in the first five minutes.
❑ *Be brief.* Don't allow anyone (especially yourself) to speak for more than two minutes at a time. Use a stop watch.
❑ *Don't allow people to drink coffee.* Meetings should be an opportunity for an exchange of ideas and plans and for coordinating actions, not for turning your meeting room into a Viennese cafeteria.

Meetings between client and consultant are a necessity. As with any cooperative effort, regular communication is a primary requirement for success. Meetings are not productive tools. They don't create or invent anything. Individuals do. Meetings are primarily control and monitoring communication tools, and as such, should be used only when necessary. The purpose of progress meetings is to facilitate periodical checks on the project progress, allow making, communicating and implementing of decisions on corrective measures and actions if the unexpected occurs or the project gets delayed or goes over budget.

Before you request a meeting or are invited to a meeting with a consultant, remember the bottom line: while in the meeting, you won't be able to work on creative and results-producing tasks. Then ask yourself a simple question: 'Is this meeting really necessary?'

Every meeting between a client and a consultant is a mutual evaluation session. Both parties watch for each other's reactions and clues to each other's behaviour. What interests the other party? What makes them nervous or relaxed? What are their objectives? Do they feel uneasy about certain issues?

Since almost 80 per cent of everything we hear is forgotten in just *two* days, detailed note-taking or recording the meetings is critical. Important thoughts, ideas, agreements and commitments may be lost if memory is relied upon. Minutes from each meeting have to be promptly typed up and distributed to the attendees and all interested parties, so they don't become outdated by subsequent events before distribution. Minutes should be clear, concise, accurate, specific and action-oriented.

Progress Meeting Review Sheet
❏ Are the meetings necessary?
❏ Are they useful?
❏ Are meetings held at the right intervals?
❏ Are they of the right length?
❏ Does the scheduled time suit those who attend?
❏ Do people who should attend the meetings attend?
❏ Are the agenda and format appropriate?
❏ Is all necessary information available?
❏ Are effective decision-making procedures in place?
❏ Are the physical/ergonomic/environmental factors satisfactory?
❏ Are the meetings recorded appropriately?
❏ Are the minutes produced of high quality (clear, concise, relevant)?
❏ Are they distributed to everybody concerned on time?
❏ Are there any interruptions? How can those interruptions be minimised?
❏ Who chairs the meetings? Is that role clearly defined?

Communicating your standards

Most problems between consultants and clients begin when the consultant has to guess at the client's quality standards, expectations, formal and informal rules, policies and procedures. If management engages in doubletalk, passing the buck or baloney, consultants very soon assume 'That's the way they operate in this company. We can do the same.' In other words, many consultants tend to assume the norms, standards and behavioural patterns of the client's organisation. And those standards and codes of conduct are not likely to be very good, otherwise the organisations wouldn't need consultants, would they?

A golden rule to keep in mind when talking to other people, and especially to consultants, who will charge you for their time, is to let them know what you expect from them and what will be used to measure their performance. Don't keep them guessing. Although some consultants are very skilful at mind-reading, most aren't psychics. Spell it out initially, and then keep reminding them of that bottom line.

Define your terms

'I don't know what you mean by "glory",' Alice said.
Humpty Dumpty smiled contemptuously, 'Of course you don't –

*till I tell you. I meant "there's a nice knockdown argument for
you"!'*

*'But "glory" doesn't mean "a nice knockdown argument",' Alice
objected.*

*'When I use a word,' Humpty Dumpty said in rather a scornful
tone, 'it means just what I choose it to mean – neither more nor less.'*

*'The question is,' said Alice, 'whether you can make words mean
different things.'*

Lewis Carroll, *Through the Looking-Glass*

The basis for any effective communication between a client and a
consultant is a proper and successful definition of terms. Assuming that
a consultant understands your views, wishes and goals is an open
invitation to misunderstandings and possible disputes. The onus is on
you, the client, to define your terms. When you say 'Send me regular
progress reports on a fortnightly basis', do you think the consultant has
received a clear and effective message? It certainly sounds like it. Let's
see.

1. What do you want? Progress reports. Clear and precise.
2. How often? Regularly, every two weeks. Clear and precise.
3. How are they to be sent? Phone, fax, normal mail, certified mail,
   pigeon mail, telex, on a floppy disc, smoke signals? Problem 1!
4. What will these reports include? Tasks performed, problems
   encountered, future issues to be resolved, hours worked, costs
   incurred? Problem 2!
5. Is the consultant to send a bill, requesting progress payment for the
   work done during that fortnight, together with the report, or later,
   after you approve all the costs? Problem 3!

We have already found three fundamental problems with your simple
message. There are quite a few more, once we get down to a detailed
level, but for illustration purposes this should suffice. The main point to
remember is to explain explicitly what you mean by project report,
progress report, improvement, simplification or any other term you may
use.

Say you request a project plan from a consultant. To him, a project
plan may mean a few bar graphs on a piece of A4 paper. To you, it may
mean a detailed list of tasks, together with their duration, resources
needed, mutual dependencies, main deliverables, major milestones,
hours needed for each activity or task and much more. Who is right and
who is wrong in this case? Even a judge wouldn't be able to decide. The
courts are full of clients and consultants suing each other for unfulfilled
promises. Many of these cases simply cannot be resolved, due to the lack

of defined standards. What is reasonable to one party may be totally unacceptable to another.

Express your views – make them understand your point of view

> Beware of the man who knows the answer before he understands the question.
>
> C.M. Manasco

When managing consultants and contractors you must be candid, frank and objective. Eliminating obstacles such as your personal feelings and your ego is one of the prerequisites for successful project management.

By definition, consultants are outsiders. They look at things and issues from that perspective and are more attuned to outside-in thinking. You, as the insider, obviously use an inside-out approach. The two should complement each other and result in a synergetic symbiosis, which will consist of the best of both worlds. In other words, you and the consultant should complement each other and help each other to see the same things from a different perspective.

Let them know that your time is valuable

Many consultants have no respect for their clients' time. Their natural tendency is to get carried away and assume that the client is always available to clarify issues or provide further guidance. While at your premises, consultants usually work on a single assignment, while clients may have half a dozen or more significant projects going on at the same time. There is obvious potential here for a conflict of time and interest.

The famous 'open door' policy, while it has certain merits and advantages, also becomes a general invitation to frequent interruptions. You'll have to make your personal policy on that issue known and reinforce it indiscriminately.

Smart move

Be as brief and precise as possible. That way you project a message which tells consultants: 'I value my time. I don't want to waste it. I also value and respect your time, because I pay for it, and I don't want to waste it. So, let's get down to business as soon as possible and keep moving towards our goal.'

Let them know your expectations

Although some experienced professionals can interpret clients' words, actions and body language, most are not good at discovering what clients expect of them. It is your task to communicate your expectations clearly:

- ❏ Solve my problems. Make my life easier and make me look good in the eyes of others.
- ❏ Speak my language. Level with me and become a part of my team. Don't talk down to me.
- ❏ Teach me in the process. Help me learn and grow.
- ❏ Avoid surprises. Be predictable and trustworthy, make me feel comfortable.
- ❏ Don't tell me what I cannot do. Tell me how to do what I want to do or what has to be done.
- ❏ Take the initiative. Display leadership and take action.
- ❏ Innovate. Offer options, new and better ways of doing things.
- ❏ Be honest and sincere. Tell me what is wrong and what is right and how to make those wrongs into rights.
- ❏ Be reasonable. If you charge first-class fees, provide first-class services.
- ❏ Keep confidential issues confidential. Establish trust.
- ❏ Pay attention to my needs. Treat me like a person, not a file.
- ❏ Give it your best shot.
- ❏ Show sincere interest in my problems. Be seen, talk to people, ask questions, give them answers.
- ❏ Deliver the goods on time and within budget. Deliver what you promised you would. Close that credibility gap.

Mental Exercise
What is the consultant's fatal mistake?
a. Asking dumb questions, which will make his lack of knowledge or understanding of the client's business obvious?
b. Not asking questions at all?
c. Asking superficial, general questions which are designed to impress less astute and more gullible clients but which alienate the more seasoned ones?

Know the answers to their questions

> *The uncreative mind can spot wrong answers, but it takes a creative mind to spot wrong questions.*
>
> A. Jay

Defining the problem or the issue is always the first step in every consulting engagement. To get a clear picture about clients' needs and the whole

Smart consultants' questions
- ❑ When do you plan to start the project?
- ❑ What is the objective of the assignment?
- ❑ When does the project have to be completed?
- ❑ Who would I report to?
- ❑ What results do you expect us to achieve?
- ❑ Who will be working with me?
- ❑ Who could answer the questions I might have?
- ❑ Has your budget been approved?

assignment, consultants need information. The main information-gathering tool at the consultant's disposal is one or more interviews with a client. In contrast to job interviews, these interviews are not formal exchanges of facts, views and opinions. They are organised, practised consultation routines. Their main purpose is to learn the client's views and understanding of a problem or situation and to broadly define the issue.

These routines are usually very casual, deliberately made that way so clients won't feel threatened, rushed or interrogated. They are purposely designed to make clients comfortable, simply because consultants have found that apporach to be the most effective.

It is normal and customary for the consultant to control the pace, the format and the length of the consultation interview, because in most cases he has a pretty good idea about what information is needed and why. Consultants experienced in their field quickly learn what type of questions must be asked of the client in order to get enough details for the draft project proposal.

Negotiating with consultants

> *The worst time to negotiate about anything is when you are in a hurry, you're tired, you've just been fighting, you're sexually aroused, you've something important on your mind, you're bored stiff, or you want to be somewhere else.*
>
> Gavin Kennedy, *Everything is Negotiable*

Your objectives
There are two major objectives in any negotiating process:

1. To change the consultant's impression of the strength of your position;

2. To change the consultant's impression of the strength of his position.

The main obstacle to achieving these two goals is the client's attitude. Many still believe that negotiation is based on competition, and try to avoid it at any cost. They either don't want to deal with a conflict or they assume an aggressive approach, based on a notion that for one party to win, the other side must lose. This competitive approach to negotiating is not very productive. The better way is a more collaborative one.

As in any other negotiating situation, both sides will try to psych out the other and determine their state of mind, intent, plans and strategies. The client has obvious advantages – he knows about bids from the consultant's competitors, can compare the proposals and quotes and certainly knows his own intentions.

The objective of the negotiating process is clear and obvious. The client is trying to get the lowest price and the best services possible, while the consultant is trying to get the highest possible price for those services. The outcome usually falls somewhere between the two. The negotiating frames of mind are illustrated in Fig. 5.1.

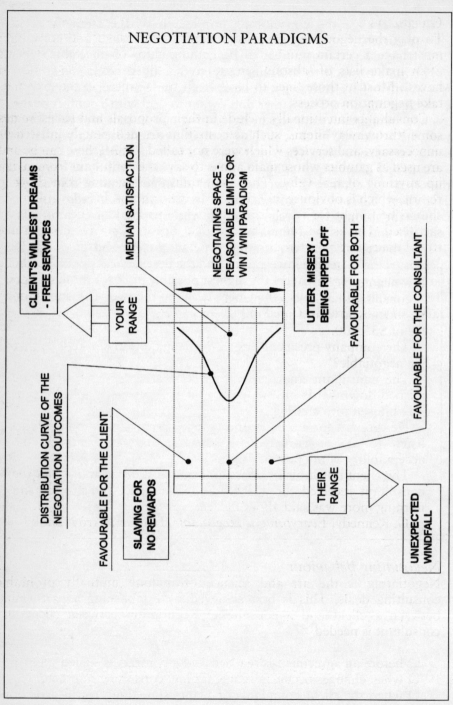

FIG. 5.1

Giveaways

To play the negotiating game successfully, both client and consultant must have a certain number of bargaining chips on the table. Clients often make lists of 'absolute must haves', 'must haves' and 'nice to haves'. Most of those 'nice to haves' can be sacrificed in the give-and-take negotiation process.

Consultants intentionally include in their proposals and fee estimates some 'throwaway' items, such as costs that are deliberately inflated or unnecessary, and services which were not called for. All these can be and are used as gambits whose main aim is to save the consultant from giving up anything of real value. The client thinks he's getting something in return, which is obviously not the case. Kings, queens, bishops and rooks should be fought for wholeheartedly, while pawns can occasionally be sacrificed. This is the rule of the prudent negotiator. Give up on some trivial issues but fight ferociously for the important ones.

Is it negotiable?
A consultant had just completed a 10-minute presentation on how he thought he could solve the client's distribution problems, for a fee of $35,000.

The company president leaned over the table and asked: 'Is that fee negotiable?'

The consultant knew that if he answered 'yes' he would be pushed downwards on the fee, and if he answered 'no' he might box himself into a corner.

He thought for a second and replied: 'I am always prepared to listen to any constructive suggestions that will improve the acceptability of my proposals.'

The client noted his response and said nothing. A week later the consultant received the go-ahead to commence the project and nothing more was said about his fee.

G. Kennedy, *Everything is Negotiable*, London, Arrow Books

Negotiating behaviour

Negotiating is the art and science of making mutually profitable consulting deals. This is best achieved by establishing a partnership between a client and a consultant. Negotiation between client and consultant is needed

- ❑ before an agreement is reached and a contract is signed
- ❑ when changes occur, in scope, timing, consulting rates, etc.
- ❑ when the client complains or wants something rectified or done differently or more urgently

Negotiation makes consultants work harder for their fees and promotes a price war between consulting firms. It helps competitive and efficient firms to become even stronger and more efficient and makes it difficult for the uncompetitive and inefficient ones to stay in business. By being a tough negotiator you also help in weeding the consulting garden!

Negotiating Tips and Tricks
- ❏ Determine your needs, desired outcomes and priorities.
- ❏ Identify the consultant's needs and estimate his priorities.
- ❏ Identify the negotiating positions and assumptions of both sides.
- ❏ Decide on possible trade-offs, should they become necessary.
- ❏ Identify ranges for negotiation.
- ❏ Start negotiating at the top of your range and push towards the bottom of their range.
- ❏ Base your negotiating strategy on the expectations of the other party.
- ❏ Negotiation is not a win/lose process. It should be a win/win situation, where both parties get most of what they want.
- ❏ Develop your own negotiating style and make good use of it.
- ❏ Never accept the first offer. The lack of negotiation will leave both parties unhappy. If you accept the terms offered by a consultant, he will think: 'I could have charged more. They are getting a good deal. That's why they accepted it so quickly.' Some time later, when the excitement of the moment is gone, you will also start thinking: 'I accepted his terms too quickly. Maybe I could have got more for my money.'
- ❏ Don't be concerned about time. The party who rushes into the negotiating process usually gives in to the other party's demands. Take as long as you need, stay calm and composed.
- ❏ The balance of power is very rarely shifted in favour of one party from the beginning. Both negotiating parties have got some power, otherwise there would be no negotiation, just orders, blackmailing and exploitation. Later in the negotiating process, the balance of power changes in favour of the stronger and more skilful negotiator.

Mental exercise
You have been left waiting outside the consultant's office for almost an hour. What do you do?
a. Make as many phone calls as you can, preferably long-distance ones?
b. Try to charm a good-looking receptionist and arrange a date?
c. Read two-year-old magazines in the waiting room.
d. Advise his secretary to tell him to come and see you in your office, because your time is valuable.

Chapter 6: Focus on Clients

Dealing with consultants is a multifaceted business. To effectively utilise their capabilities, to manage the resources at your disposal, to stay in control at all times and ultimately to reach your goals, you'll need a myriad skills and detailed knowledge of certain disciplines and techniques.

Analysing yourself

There are two things every manager thinks he's good at – interviewing and selecting consultants, and working with them. Both are quite confidential and important activities, yet not many people discuss them or learn from each other the secrets of the trade. Despite the range of training courses and seminars on almost every business, technical and management topic imaginable, courses on how to manage consultants are still very rare.

Just as consultants' skills, experience and attitudes determine the failure or success of projects, so do the client's skills and attitudes. There are two sides to every coin, and your head will be on one of them.

The art of managing consultants can be learned and mastered, providing you first learn about yourself and your strengths and weaknesses, and master your own emotions, attitudes and methods.

'Soft' Skills

We were all taught in school to use logic, reason and facts in our chosen careers. Rules, procedures, logical reasoning and vertical thinking were emphasised, while feelings, intuition, hunch and serendipity were downgraded in value, if mentioned at all. In our scholastic lives there was no room for intuition. In our real lives, both left-brain analysis and right-brain intuition are used.

Management isn't and shouldn't be an exception. Just as relying solely on feelings and intuition in managing consultants would be a recipe for disaster, using only objective and logical tools and evaluating methods would deprive clients of many invaluable and sometimes crucial supportive mechanisms.

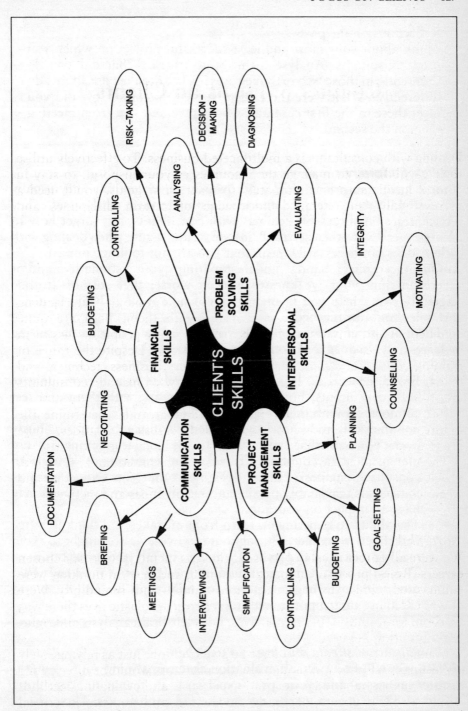

FIG. 6.1

> **Reflections on the past**
> Think about your most and least successful project on which you
> used consultants. Analyse them. Study them. What did you do
> differently in those two extreme cases? What did the consultants do
> differently? What were the critical success factors? How did you
> meet these in the first case and what prevented you from meeting
> them in the second?

Skills of a lonely client

People have a surprising tendency towards self-deception. They usually
overestimate their strengths and underestimate their weaknesses. They
concentrate on successful dealings with consultants, but forget how to
deal properly with themselves. Being smart and astute when dealing with
others does not necessarily mean that you are not fooling yourself.

On the other hand, underestimating your strengths and/or
overestimating your weaknesses is even worse; that sort of attitude
certainly won't help you in managing consultants. As always in life, a
balance should be reached.

There are three groups of skills you'll need as a user of consulting
services and a manager of consulting projects:

1. Broad, general skills, such as how to relate to and communicate
   with consultants, how to treat them, work with them and feel
   comfortable with them.
2. Specific skills and knowledge needed on your job. This obviously
   doesn't mean that you have to be an accountant to use
   management accounting firms or an engineer to deal with
   consulting engineers, but it does mean that you should learn as
   much as is reasonably possible about other disciplines which may
   have an impact on your job.
3. The ability to experiment, learn from mistakes and think in a free
   and effective manner. Throughout our lives, we are taught to avoid
   making mistakes, to play it safe and go quietly about our business.
   That's the most damaging school of thought one can attend. That
   rationale leaves us unprepared for failures in life and unable to
   capitalise on temporary setbacks.

Self-evaluation sheets and how to use them

Below you will find two self-evaluation sheets analysing your strengths
and weaknesses and your past experience in managing consulting
projects. There are no marks, no pass or fail percentages. These sheets
are for your eyes only. Whatever you do, be honest with yourself.

Nobody else will see your self-assessment.

Feel free to photocopy these pages. Keep your sheets in your personal folder in a safe place. As you make progress and improve your skills and/or eliminate your weaknesses you can change them or fill in new ones. You can create your own sheets if you find the enclosed ones unsuitable, or add your own strengths and weaknesses at the bottom of the sheets.

Use a separate sheet for each major project you have done or for a group of smaller, interrelated jobs. Again, you can customise this sheet to suit your preferences, or create your own. In this case, form is not important, essence is.

When analysing and 'classifying' your past tasks, experiences and achievements, try to group them and evaluate them on the basis of critical factors such as initiative, integrity, ability to learn, adaptability, planning and control, attention to detail, work standards, etc. For example, some of the more important cases would be:

- ❑ When you achieved more than you expected
- ❑ When you failed despite giving your best
- ❑ When you succeeded because you persisted for a period of time
- ❑ When you successfully implemented consultants' recommendations or ideas
- ❑ When you successfully implemented your own ideas
- ❑ When you made a difficult decision
- ❑ When you did more than was required
- ❑ When you failed/succeeded because of poor/proper planning
- ❑ When you felt you could have done a better job

When you finish your objective analysis, identify your mistakes and the areas for improvement.

Client's Self-Evaluation Sheet
Mark [✓] or [✗] as applicable

My strengths and assets	My weaknesses and handicaps
❑ Good communication skills	❑ Poor communication/briefing skills
❑ Willing to learn	❑ No experience in managing projects
❑ Able to work under pressure	❑ No experience in managing consultants
❑ Takes initiative	❑ Unable to say no
❑ Reliable and responsible	❑ Not assertive enough
❑ Flexible	❑ Lack of negotiating skills
❑ Cooperative/easy to work with	❑ Unable to understand broader concepts
❑ Persistent	❑ Poor planning skills
❑ Decisive	❑ Poor interviewing and selection skills
❑ Able to delegate	❑ Unsystematic and inefficient
❑ Thorough (attention to detail)	❑ Lack of planning
❑ Innovative _____	❑ _____
❑ _____	❑ _____
❑ _____	❑ _____
❑ _____	❑ _____

Previous Project Experience Analysis Sheet

❏ Project:

❏ Initial problem:

❏ Task:

❏ Approach:

❏ Outcome (results):

❏ Accomplishments:

❏ Mistakes made:

❏ Causes of those mistakes:

❏ Lessons learned:

Learning from consultants and your own mistakes

Learning is not a continuously rising process. It goes up, then down and levels off at a plateau. Then it starts going up again. The objective of lifelong learning should be to pull up to a slightly higher plateau every time you complete a cycle of ups and downs.

Through their eyes only

How are you perceived by consultants? Which stereotype do you resemble? Which pigeonhole have they put you in? If you're not sure, ask them. The truth is delicate, but insist on it. It may help you to become aware of your weaknesses and to start using your assets to your advantage. While your own employees normally wouldn't tell you the truth, many consultants will.

Consulting is a double-edged sword

Egotism and egoism are the most common human commodities. I, me, my and mine are the four most spoken words in every language. As a manager, you want to look good in the eyes of your superiors, to earn respect and obedience from your subordinates. You want to be perceived as resourceful, competent, energetic, innovative. You aspire to be a top troubleshooter, maverick, motivator. And the fact of the matter is, you can be all that, and more. How? By ceasing to be inward-bound. By turning outward, and using the often overlooked resource, the one every manager has plenty of: other people. They can make you whatever you want to be, if you know how to use them efficiently in the process of attaining your goals.

Good managers surround themselves with smart, industrious, capable people. These assistants evaluate their bosses' ideas, suggest improvements and provide recommendations. Top managers go one step further. They hire people who will generate ideas for them. They are usually called consultants. All the street-smart manager does is pick the winning idea, then gets the consultant to analyse the issue and make a recommendation. Once he gets the green light, the recommendations are implemented, and, if the idea turns out to be a success, the manager takes the credit and enormously strengthens his position and influence.

The reversal of fortunes is also a possiblity. How many managers have looked incompetent, irresponsible, ill-informed, careless and plain no good by using consultants who were incompetent, irresponsible, ill-informed, careless and plain no good? Many!

Using consultants is a double-edged sword. It can cut both ways. Just like any tool or weapon, if you handle it with care and take some basic precautions, it will serve you well and pay for its cost many times over.

The mistakes clients make

Failing to set clear goals and objectives

Apart from the main objectives of an assignment, think about secondary, *en route* objectives, the ones that could be cost-effectively achieved along the way, either because they are related in some way to the main goal, or because their achievement is a natural follow-on from the main project.

Learning objectives are often overlooked benefits that can be harnessed to each project, be it successful or not. The main aim behind learning objectives, for you and your team, is to acquire enough knowledge to be able to do a similar job next time around, either by yourselves or with reduced consultant input.

Cloning themselves

The cloning effect is the tendency among clients to hire consultants they understand, trust, feel comfortable with and who are the most predictable to them. In short, people like themselves.

They are looking for people with whom they have a fair chance of getting along, communicating well and sharing common values. They try to multiply themselves by hiring people with similar backgrounds, from the same part of the country, of the same gender and age group. The only problem with this approach is that inadequacies are duplicated and the lack of breadth and depth of knowledge and experience is accentuated even further.

Following bad advice

There are two groups of consultants who should be avoided like the plague. Some are well-meaning but hopelessly incompetent people. Some consultants, on the other hand, are unethical, low-integrity predators who either try to 'sell' prepacked solutions or deliberately make their assignments last as long as possible. Either way, if you blindly follow their advice, recommendations and 'solutions', you lose.

Nobody wants to be a loser, yet many clients accept and follow anything their advisers serve to them. The practice of seeking a second opinion is still in its infancy in the consulting business.

If you are not happy with your doctor, or if you doubt his diagnosis and recommendations, you ask for another doctor's opinion. Two heads are usually better than one (unless they are both incompetent). You have the same rights when using consulting services.

Mental Exercise
What are the two most important words in dealing with consultants?
a) If only . . .   b) What if . . .   c) How much . . . d) How long . . .

Looking for the magic wand

The human search for miracles, short cuts and universal remedies is a never-ending story. King Arthur's knights searched for the Holy Grail, alchemists spent their lives trying to find a way of turning ordinary metals into gold and project managers spend hours and days trying to find a foolproof way to control consultants, projects and costs.

The panacea, universal recipe, magic wand or anything similar is pure and simple wishful thinking. Some clients think that consultants are there to solve any problem they may have. All they have to do is pick up the phone, arrange a meeting, give a quick briefing, and off the consultant merrily goes to deliver the solution some time later. If you belong to this group, you still have some growing up to do.

Expecting too much too soon

Dear God, I pray for patience. And I want it right now.

Oren Arnold

One of the most prominent characteristics of modern-day Western management is its impatience with slow, gradual improvements, changes and developments. Results are expected overnight and quantum leaps are striven for. Clients sometimes expect the same from consultants working for them, and those unrealistic expectations and lack of sustained commitment to gradual change are two main causes of frustration (on both sides), tension and misunderstanding.

Another common problem amongst project managers and clients who deal with consultants is their lack of understanding of how and at what pace results are produced. Most people think in linear terms, which assume constant and proportional achievement of goals during the whole life of a project. This certainly isn't the case with most projects.

Achievement doesn't necessarily follow effort. Through years of research and comparisons, management experts have concluded that, on average, during the initial and final phases of projects, increased effort results in smaller increases in achievement, compared to the midlife of a project, where the relationship between effort and achievement is more or less linear. This observation has been named 'the S-curve' and is illustrated in Fig. 6.2.

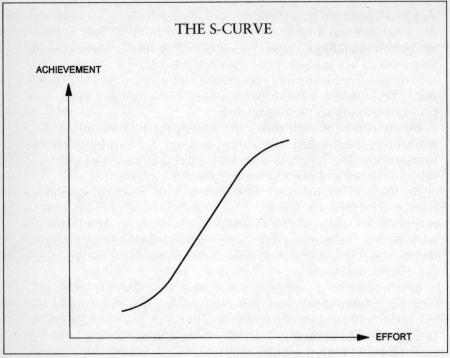

FIG. 6.2

Falling for current fads

Fishbone diagrams, TGC, TPM, TQM, MBO, Theory-Z, MBWA and other management recipes for success are being portrayed by both clients and consultants as the pinnacles of the misnamed management science. Misnamed because management is not a science, no matter how hard graduate-school professors try to emphasise the hardcore techniques of the quantitative world. There is no science that is in any way specific to management and there is no technique that works every time and in every company.

In their quest for a universal management tool, one that can solve problems, motivate and reward, improve productivity and competitiveness, cut costs and maximise profits, managers are all too quick to embrace any idea management consultants come up with. The fact that previous attempts to implement other fads have failed miserably doesn't seem to discourage them from trying again. The only tangible results achieved by those current theories are increased sales of management books and the flourishing of the management consulting profession.

Zen and Quantum leap theory

An American and a Japanese company were building two high-rise apartment buildings, next to each other, for a developer in Singapore. They started about the same time. By the end of the first month, the Americans had cleared the site and finished testing the soil. The Japanese were drawing boxes and arranging tasks on a project-planning software package.

By the end of month three, the Americans had mobilised their workforce, established the camp and started working on the foundations. The Japanese were busy talking to suppliers and local subcontractors and negotiating purchasing agreements.

By the end of month six, the American building started to emerge. The Japanese lot was quiet – there was no sign of activity, except occasional visits by various delegations and project groups who would measure, plan, walk around and consult among themselves. That would start cynical comments from the American supervisors and workers.

By the end of month nine, the American firm faced its first setbacks. Material was late, rains delayed big concrete works and industrial problems emerged over leave and award conditions. The Japanese had built their camp and started foundation work. By the end of the first year, the Americans were still deadlocked in disputes with suppliers and unions. They called in consultants and industrial relations experts. The Japanese building was progressing at a modest but steady pace. The American building was still half finished. By the end of month fifteen, the Japanese building was finished. The American skyscraper stayed half finished, much to the amazement of quality-control experts and management consultants.

Not seeing the obvious

> *The obscure we eventually see. The completely obvious, it seems, takes longer.*
>
> Edward R. Murrow

An important letter has been stolen. After numerous painstaking searches, the police are unable to find it. Detective C. Auguste Dupin realises that the prime suspect, a government minister, could have eluded the police by not hiding the letter at all but by leaving it in plain sight all the time! Because of their preconceived notion that the letter must have been concealed in a secret place, they were not able to see it.

This was the plot of Edgar Allan Poe's short story 'The Purloined

Letter'. The plots of many unsuccessful projects, which are based on wrong decisions and improper actions, are very similar – both clients and consultants fail to see the obvious.

Failing to be consistent and predictable

Trust is the basis for every successful client–consultant relationship, and consistency and predictability help establish trust. Each party knows that the other side will always act, behave and think the way they expect them to and the way they are used to. Imagine the confusion in your consultant's mind if you require certain standards today and something completely different tomorrow. Your professionalism has to be based on consistency, predictability and trust. Whimsical attitudes and undefined standards and rules won't do either your professional image or your business any good.

Failing to establish emotional bonds with consultants

Consulting is an intimate business. You talk to consultants working for you. You rub shoulders with them, you work with them. You listen to them, their suggestions, opinions, requests. You discover their personalities, attitudes, potential and limitations. You become a vital part of their lives and they become an important part of yours. No matter who they are, they will all want a client who will listen empathically, who will avoid appearing superior, domineering or pushy and who will not pass judgement on them all the time.

Obviously, this doesn't mean that you have to become good friends with consultants working for you. A close working relationshp based on respect and fairness will go a long way.

Forgetting why consultants were hired

A consultant's advice will be judged not by his intentions and efforts, but by your results at the end of the exercise. This is a simple law of reality. Never forget why you hired a consultant in the first place – to help you achieve something. The bottom line is that everything you do should contribute to that bottom line and help him achieve as much as possible. It is very easy to go off at a tangent and lose sight of your aims and goals. It happens to some consultants as well. Don't let it happen, because it will cost you at the end.

You should not only determine whether the consultant has delivered what the contract specified, but also whether the end result or product satisfies your original need or solves the original problem and whether that result or product is of acceptable quality.

Your priorities
What aspects of a typical consulting assignment are more important to you and which do you perceive as less significant? List your priorities here:
❑ Costs
❑ Time schedule
❑ Quality
❑ Client–consultant relationship
❑ Legal protection and cover
❑ Consultant's methods and approach
❑ Favourable impressions on top management

Bringing out dirty laundry

Criticising, condemning or complaining about your company, its business, plans and directions, its competitors and customers, your superiors or your subordinates, in the presence of or directly to consultants is an unhealthy habit and a risky business.

If they label you as an unmotivated, disloyal, frustrated individual, who doesn't think much of your employer's business and your own role in it, they will consciously or unconsciously put in less effort and deliver service of a lesser quality.

Your actions and behaviour are constantly being observed, analysed and interpreted not only by your superiors, colleagues and subordinates, but also by people outside your organisation, such as consultants, suppliers, contractors, competitors and customers.

Smart move
Never go 'off the record'. It's risky and unnecessary. Stick to the rules and avoid unpleasant surprises. Also, never bad-mouth your employers, especially not in front of consultants.

Asking for advice, but not taking it

To profit from good advice requires more wisdom than to give it.
J. Collins

Consultants get paid for the advice given to clients, not for the advice taken by clients. This is where a big problem stems from. Many clients, for whatever reason, just don't take the advice, don't implement the solutions and recommendations given by consultants or don't follow up with the actions needed to make assignments succeed.

Asking consultants to justify a decision already made

Have you noticed how the most avid readers of automotive magazines are people who have just bought a car? Or how some managers hire consultants just to endorse a decision that has already been made? In both cases, what people need is to reassure themselves that their choice is valid and that the decision made was a sound one.

Sometimes there's more to it than simply confirming and justifying the client's actions. This way it seems that decisions were made and implemented by the consultants, not the management, who get out with clean hands. It is a plot commonly used in downsizing, restructuring and other unpopular programmes where workers are retrenched or affected in some other significant way.

Being a perfectionist, not a compromiser

> Compromise is the art of dividing a cake in such a way that everybody believes they've got the biggest piece.

Quite often the solution to a particular problem is not the ideal one; in many cases it is simply the lesser of two or more wrongs, the one with the fewest negatives attached to it. A project manager has to learn to live with that kind of imperfection. Perfectionism costs time and money and seldom achieves results.

A perfectionist never achieves much. He waits and procrastinates, never accepting that some problems simply cannot be solved. They have to be accepted and lived with. A compromiser, on the other hand, doesn't wait for conditions or timing to be perfect, because he knows they'll never be.

Don't wait for perfect conditions or until you have all the information you need to make a decision, because you'll be waiting a long time. Take actions based on sufficient information and reasonable risks. Do something, but whatever you do, don't be a perfectionist. It is always better to make a decision, even if it later proves to be the wrong one, than not to make it at all. Indecisiveness and 'playing it safe' should be treated as one's worst enemies, because they are. They bring stagnation instead of progress, status quo instead of new ideas and improvements.

Putting the cart before the horse

Many clients start from the wrong end of the rope by getting into motion without stating the objectives and then turning back and working out the steps in reverse. They simply go through the motions of engaging a consultant, without a clear understanding of what it is they are trying to achieve, hoping that the ultimate goals and aims will crystallise out at some stage. They also expect quantum leaps that will rapidly take them to the solutions, without properly defining the causes. What they don't realise is that small, incremental steps, following a planned path, will ultimately lead to improvement, because whatever can be done, can be done better.

Success secrets

Assign employees to work with consultants

When delegating tasks and assigning roles to those of your employees who will be working on a project with consultants, you have to make sure they do what they are supposed to. You cannot rely on consultants to do this, because it isn't their job, and in most cases they don't want to create any ill-feeling by pointing out the individuals, groups or departments who are not cooperating or pulling their weight.

Your employees are your responsibility. Make sure they know what is expected of them, how to do what you want them to do and which criteria will be used to evaluate their performance on the project.

Don't just assign your own employees to work with consultants, make a conscious effort and conduct a brief introductory session with each one of them. Find out their expectations. Identify what motivates or demotivates them to participate in the project, and which functions and tasks they prefer doing. Ask for their advice, views and feelings about the whole project.

Provide the consultants with all the information you have available

This point may sound trivial, but some managers have an unhealthy habit of withholding certain information from consultants. The reasons may vary. In some cases, managers try to cover up their flaws and past mistakes, omissions and errors of judgement. This is a common reason for deliberately withholding information. In other instances, they don't realise the importance of certain information or its relevance to the project in progress. This may be called 'unconscious withholding'.

Another example of deliberate withholding of relevant information is the 'let's see how smart they are and leave it to them to discover what's going on' game, which is not only unnecessary and unprofessional, but costs money. Games are for kindergarten kids, not for project management professionals.

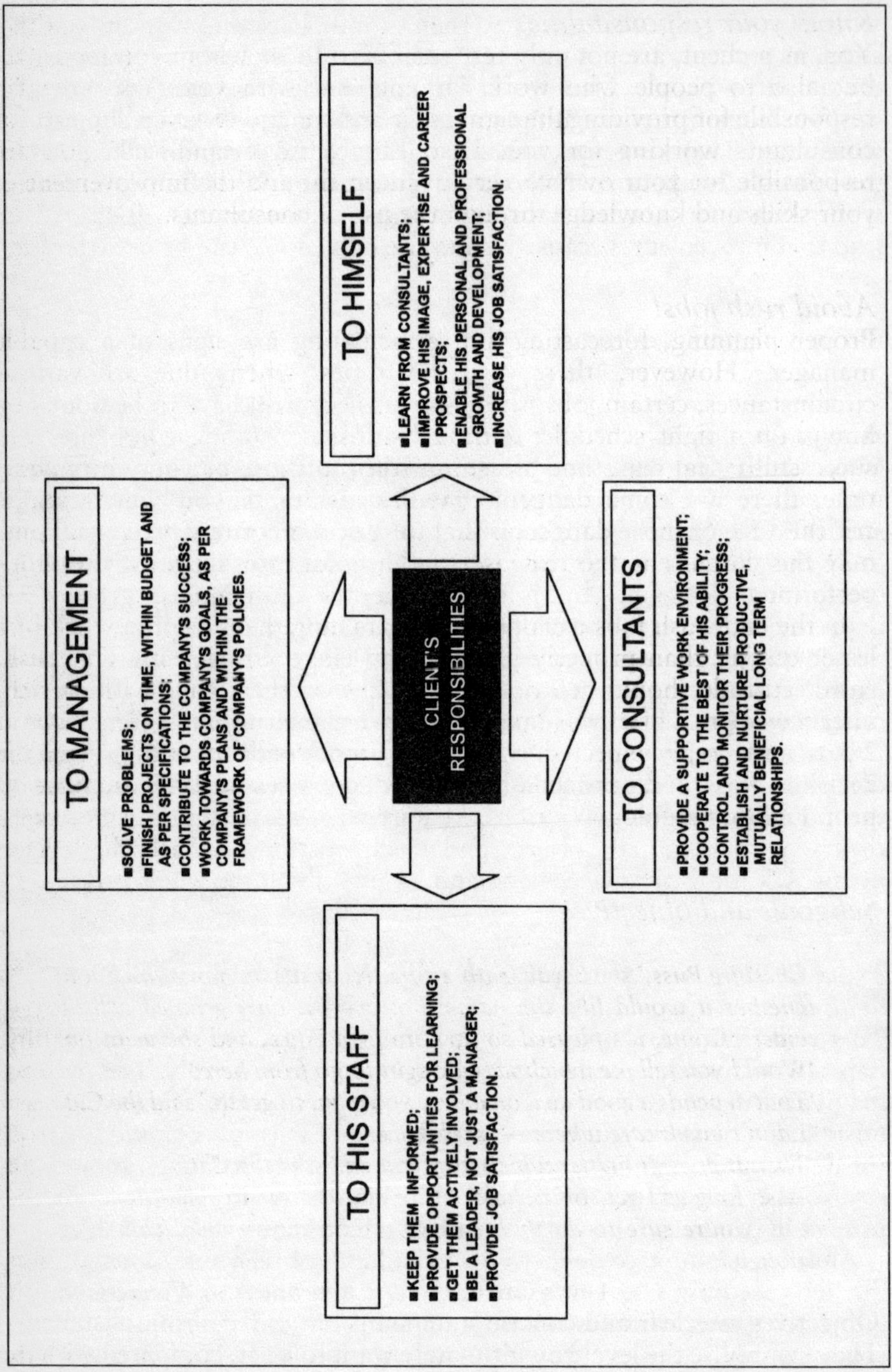

TO HIMSELF

- LEARN FROM CONSULTANTS;
- IMPROVE HIS IMAGE, EXPERTISE AND CAREER PROSPECTS;
- ENABLE HIS PERSONAL AND PROFESSIONAL GROWTH AND DEVELOPMENT;
- INCREASE HIS JOB SATISFACTION.

TO MANAGEMENT

- SOLVE PROBLEMS;
- FINISH PROJECTS ON TIME, WITHIN BUDGET AND AS PER SPECIFICATIONS;
- CONTRIBUTE TO THE COMPANY'S SUCCESS;
- WORK TOWARDS COMPANY'S GOALS, AS PER COMPANY'S PLANS AND WITHIN THE FRAMEWORK OF COMPANY'S POLICIES.

CLIENT'S RESPONSIBILITIES

TO CONSULTANTS

- PROVIDE A SUPPORTIVE WORK ENVIRONMENT;
- COOPERATE TO THE BEST OF HIS ABILITY;
- CONTROL AND MONITOR THEIR PROGRESS;
- ESTABLISH AND NURTURE PRODUCTIVE, MUTUALLY BENEFICIAL LONG TERM RELATIONSHIPS.

TO HIS STAFF

- KEEP THEM INFORMED;
- PROVIDE OPPORTUNITIES FOR LEARNING;
- GET THEM ACTIVELY INVOLVED;
- BE A LEADER, NOT JUST A MANAGER;
- PROVIDE JOB SATISFACTION.

FIG 6.3

Know your responsibilities

You, as a client, are not only responsible to those whom you report to, but also to people who work for you and with you. You are also responsbile for providing the right environment and constant support for consultants working for you. Last, but by no means least, you are responsible for your own career advancement and the improvement of your skills and knowledge through the use of consultants.

Avoid rush jobs!

Proper planning, forecasting and anticipating are signs of a capable manager. However, there will be times when, due to various circumstances, certain jobs, studies or projects will have to be done in a hurry, on a tight schedule. Although most consulting companies can successfully deal with time pressure and produce results in quite a short time, there are some dangers that are always present when time is critical. One of those dangers is that, if the project runs late, consultants may cut corners at the expense of the quality or scope of the work performed.

In the end, rush jobs usually cost clients more and result in work of a lesser quality than properly planned and executed projects. The 'rush, rush!' attitude should be avoided from the outset. I have witnessed an instance where a brief was faxed to three engineering consulting firms at 2 p.m. and a reply expected by the same time the very next day, when the decision was made on the spot, based on received brief outlines of proposed methodology.

Set goals and objectives

> 'Cheshire Puss,' she began, rather timidly, as she did not at all know whether it would like the name: however, it only grinned a little wider. 'Come, it's pleased so far,' thought Alice, and she went on. 'Would you tell me which way I ought to go from here?'
> 'That depends a good deal on where you want to get to,' said the Cat.
> 'I don't much care where —' said Alice.
> 'Then it doesn't matter which way you go,' said the Cat.
> '— so long as I get somewhere,' Alice added as an explanation.
> 'Oh, you're sure to do that,' said the Cat, 'if you only walk long enough.'
>
> Lewis Carroll, *Alice's Adventures in Wonderland*

Objectives are clear and concise statements of desired accomplishments. They symbolise the level you ultimately want to be at, compared with the present level of achievement. Objectives should be:

❑ *Concise.* Keep it simple. Each goal has to be self-explanatory.

❑ *Specific.* General statements, wishes and 'nice to have' dreams won't do. The more detailed the description of your goals is, the better.

❑ *Written.* William Faulkner once said, 'I don't know what I think until I read what I said.' This may sound like a contradiction, but it is much easier to clarify, organise and systematise one's thinking and impressions by going through a written code of thoughts. This doesn't only apply to goals. It can serve for recording your 'inner voice'. The idea is simple: record as many inner thoughts, impressions, clues, leads and ideas as possible. During meetings with consultants, follow the points made and probe deeper into the clues. Writing is the most efficient and the least painful way towards clear, systematic thinking and organising your thoughts, goals and ideas.

❑ *Few in number.* Don't strive for too many things at the same time. Prioritise your goals and concentrate on achieving them one by one. Having too many objectives contradicts one of the prerequisites for success in any field: concentration of effort and definiteness of purpose. It diffuses and weakens the impact.

❑ *Realistic and relatively easy to implement.* Unrealistic goals are a very common cause of frustration and low self-esteem. Don't be too harsh on yourself. Divide major goals into smaller ones, which are easier to achieve.

❑ *Measurable.* It is very hard, almost impossible, to monitor your progress towards achieving your goals if they cannot be measured or in some other way quantified.

❑ *Time-framed.* Goals are dreams with a deadline. By positioning your goals in time you make them more realistic and measurable. You will be able to monitor your rate of progress towards achieving them.

❑ *Congruent and compatible.* All goals set should have a common denominator; they should lead you towards your ultimate purpose and they shouldn't contradict each other. The attainment of one goal should make it easier to reach the others.

❑ *Challenging and inspiring.* Objectives should bring the best out of people, both your own employees and consultants. They should provide motivation and stimulation and be a source of excitement and ignition of ideas. Good objectives force people to get out of their comfort zones, to struggle and play hard, play to win. They should be the ultimate aim of your efforts and source of your strengths.

❑ *Stable*. Once objectives are set and agreed upon by all involved parties, they should be stuck to and persisted with. Frequent changes are signs of poor planning, inadequate goal-setting and lack of persistence and resilience, and a cause of poor morale and disillusionment.

Remember, the longer and more complex the objective is, the more likely it is that the project will fail.

Get involved on a permanent and detailed basis!

The advantages of full client involvement in a project handled by consultants are numerous and quite significant from many points of view.

❑ *Confidence*. The simple fact that at any time you know what a consultant is doing, why he is doing it and roughly what the cumulative project costs are to date will make you confident in the consultant, yourself and the whole project. Insecurity and doubt stem from lack of knowledge about the current project status and the lack of client involvement. That involvement doesn't have to be on a detailed basis, where the client personally checks or knows every consultant's move, far from that. But it has to be active, ongoing and consistent.

Clients involvement is often erratic, sometimes spending days or weeks working closely with a consultant, at other times letting long periods go by without any monitoring or control whatsoever. This is obviously undesirable. The message a consultant should get is that you want to be involved in and know about every significant development, activity and problem, but not to be bothered with trivial, routine and unimportant information.

❑ *Easier and better implementation of the proposed solutions*. It is normal practice for a consultant to propose a solution to a client, without the client's understanding of how that proposed solution is to be arrived at or what factors influenced the consultant to propose that particular solution and not some other one. With the client's active and continuous involvement in finding a solution, its implementation is usually much easier and the final results more substantial compared with those achieved without the client's involvement.

❑ *Learning experience*. Apart from the obvious benefits of the consultant completing the project or solving a problem, the biggest gain for the client is in the form of new knowledge and enhanced experience, both results of the client's participation in the project. That knowledge and experience, just an indirect benefit at this stage, will unquestionably result in direct, tangible benefits in future projects or consulting assignments, because it will make the client more knowledgeable about the workings of consulting assignments and help him avoid making or repeating certain common mistakes.

Know how to deal with sensitive issues

Some issues, problems and projects can be classified as sensitive, in terms of possible consequences and problems that may arise before, during or after the implementation of the agreed solution. While the investigation is being carried out, employees may have strong feelings about it, they may feel threatened, left out, ignored or manipulated.

A typical example of such a situation would be a cost-cutting project where one of the objectives is to lower the operational costs by reducing the number of employees. In cases like these particular skill and caution is needed.

Simplify, but don't oversimplify

> The great fault all over the world in business is that people overcomplicate and forget that the main ingredients for success are common sense and simplicity. I use lawyers and accountants as little as possible.
> Peter de Savary, *Sunday Telegraph Magazine,* 8 September 1985

The real world is a complex and chaotic system. Being creatures of limited attention span and comprehension ability, we have to simplify our methods and models in order to be able to deal with problems of any nature. This simplification is most obvious in our tendency to limit the number of variables that characterise a method or a problem. The number of variables we can come to grips with is quite low – two! Although very common, this two-factor analysis quite often contributes to the creation of problems which are consequences of other variables neglected in the process.

A typical example is project management, a science and art which defines three elements as pillars of control: quality, cost and time. The two-variable theory states that while controlling two of these three variables, project managers and consultants very often neglect the third one. That third variable usually becomes uncontrolled and goes on the rampage, as in the case of escalating costs if too much attention is paid to quality and completing a project on time.

So, although necessary, simplification should be treated as a necessary evil and possible consequences reckoned with. Confucious said that men do not stumble over mountains, but over molehills. Details have an annoying and distracting tendency to accumulate, multiply and compound themselves. How does a job get delayed by a month? One day at a time.

Smart move
Any third-rate project manager can make things more complex and elaborate. The sign of a first-rate manager is simplicity. Make things simple. Decrease complexity.

Hire people smarter than you

> *Here lies a man who knew how to bring into his service men better than he was himself.*
>
> Andrew Carnegie's epitaph

Hire consultants who are smarter, more experienced and more capable than yourself. You need giants, as your logic tells you, not dwarfs, as your ego tells you. Go for first-rate people and pay first-rate fees.

Just make sure you don't make a common mistake during face-to-face meetings with consultants. The client does most of the talking and the consultant merely listens attentively and occasionally nods in important places. The more you talk and the more he listens, the smarter you'll believe him to be. This is an old trick, but one that works all the time. 'What an interesting conversation we had,' you'll say, forgetting that the other person hardly spoke a word.

Treat them with respect

> *You can buy a man's time; you can buy his physical presence at a given place; you can even buy a measured number of his skilled muscular motions per hour. But you cannot buy enthusiasm . . . You cannot buy loyalty . . . you cannot buy the devotion of hearts, minds or souls. You must earn these.*
>
> Clarence Francis

When you win an argument or negotiation, do what real winners do – leave respect behind you. Poor winners leave behind them only

---

Courtesy and respect

❏ Return consultants' phone calls promptly and professionally. Remember, it isn't only a matter of good manners; it's your money that pays for their time, so don't waste it.

❏ Notify them as soon as possible of any changes (additions, alternations, new information, budget restrictions) to the project.

❏ Treat everybody with respect. Be courteous and polite.

❏ Always talk in other people's terms. Be emphatic. Put yourself in other people's shoes.

❏ Treat every relationship as a long-term investment. Cultivate your relationships; let them grow and flourish. Be patient. Allow time for some of them to bear fruit.

❏ Avoid criticising, complaining or blaming consultants. Any fool can do that. Avoid arguments and open confrontations.

❏ Recognise consultants' efforts and praise them for a job well done. Everybody needs words of appreciation. Don't shy away from showing your satisfaction.

❏ Be friendly and approachable. Let consultants feel your respect for them and how much you value their efforts and achievements.

---

apprehension and hate. In other words, turn your adversaries into friends and allies, not into opponents and enemies.

Make them feel comfortable in their dealings with you. To do that, it is necessary for you to be comfortable with yourself. An uptight, suspicious, pessimistic client makes consultants feel the same way.

Life is a puzzle. Predicting the future is a tricky business and nobody can guarantee that you'll never deal with the same individual or consulting company again. Maybe next time you'll depend on them in some way or need something from them (a reference, vital information, a recommendation). It may even be your job that's at stake.

Make them help you become a star

> No matter how much work a man can do . . . he will not advance far
> if he cannot work through others.
>
> John Craig

There are two steps towards becoming a star. First, make sure the consultants you manage do a good job. Secondly, if they do, make sure that others in your organisation know about it and don't forget to emphasise your contribution to the success. In other words, gain visibility by marketing your achievements.

Have you ever heard of the human tendency of labelling people by association? More often than not, others will judge you by the people they associate you with. Choose your 'associates' carefully. Birds of a feather do flock together, so seek the company of influential, authoritative and successful consultants. If you are lucky, you'll be perceived as such, too. Your image is a very vulnerable commodity, so don't waste it on just anybody.

Most consulting projects you'll manage will be routine jobs of moderate importance to your employer's business. By completing those assignments successfully, you should progress through the ranks gradually and steadily. Every now and then, however, an important assignment will come up. This will be your best opportunity to show what you are made of. Whatever you do well normally, do it now even better. Select the consultant who can best help you ride that horse of success.

Fight organisational resistance

Depending on the nature of a consulting assignment, various feelings within your organisation may arise and the atmosphere within certain groups of employees may heat up. This is particularly probable in the case of projects whose goals are performance improvement, reduction in the number of employees, restructuring and reorganising of departments, introduction of new work practices or demarcation of tasks and duties.

In any assignment, the very presence of strangers in the organisation is enough to arouse suspicion, rumours, apprehension and a guarded attitude. This is often augmented by certain consulting activities, such as data-gathering from files, production, maintenance, sales and personnel records, interviews with employees, surveys and questionnaires. The workers, the unions and even the management feel threatened, so barriers are automatically erected at all levels of the corporation.

The first step in dealing with resistance is to identify what people are resisting, what they are afraid of. This, in many cases, is either change or the prospect of additional demands that may be imposed on them, forcing them to learn new skills, accept new conditions of employment, transfer, or anything of a similar nature. Resistance is therefore always linked to an avoidance of threatening conditions, either real or imagined.

It is better to manage resistance proactively by assuming it will happen and working on minimising its impact, than reacting to it when it does occur.

One of the fundamental problems in using consultants is the

resentment it quite often creates among employees. Although a manager may send a message, 'They will help us, so everybody will be better off', what the employees hear is, 'We trust and value outsiders more than we trust our own employees!'

Once employees' fears are identified, it isn't difficult to fight them. Information and participation are the two key steps in these efforts. Individuals and groups have to be informed about the project. They have to know what the goals are and what methods will be used to achieve those goals. Once the work groups are informed, their participation in some activities can be solicited. The principle of involvement is a powerful concept. It motivates individuals and gives them a sense of purpose. If left out, they become a strong opposition. If, on the other hand, they feel they *own* the process, they become collaborators and evangelists for *their* cause.

Advanced tactics

In-house consulting

> *To accept good advice is but to increase one's own ability.*
>
> Goethe

One recent trend has been the growth of internal or in-house consulting. Companies that once relied exclusively on external consultants to do most of their problem-solving are increasingly deciding to keep some of that expertise within the company.

The principal reason for decisions of this kind is monetary. Simply, the high fees charged by outside consultants precipitated the trend and forced clients to take a hard look at what value they were getting for their money, and to slash those costs by employing permanent staff who could provide if not the same, then certainly adequate service.

While in-house consulting is not a novelty in some disciplines, such as engineering and accounting, it is slowly but surely spreading to other professions, such as lawyers and management consultants.

Internal consulting groups vary in size, scope and level of expertise, depending on the company's size and the management philosophy. The *modus operandi*, however, is a common one: the consulting team is approached by a departmental manager, who becomes the client once the decision to proceed is made and the project authorised.

There are some differences between the two types of consulting. External consultants usually have more freedom to act, compared with their internal counterparts, who are, no matter how loosely, still part of the client's organisation. Internal consultants, on the other hand, are more familiar with the client's culture and the internal workings of the organisation, and appear less threatening to the employees.

There is another important advantage of using internal consulting teams. Internal consultants feel more pressure to implement the recommendations properly and successfully. They cannot simply pack up and leave, as external consultants can. Internal consultants remain attached to their solutions and have to live with the consequences of their own actions and recommendations.

Potential savings by using in-house consultants come from the elimination of four groups of costs:

1. Starting costs, which essentially cover mobilisation and learning about the client's company
2. Marketing and selling costs, which external consultants calculate into their fees
3. Reimbursable expenses, such as rental cars, hotel bills, meals, air fares, travel time (which is usually booked at full rate)
4. Contingency mark-ups, which get included in quotations to cover unpredicted problems or learning periods, but which may never eventuate

'Just-in-time' teams

Keeping optimum staff levels is a challenge and a problem that many consulting firms cannot successfully solve. If a company bases its levels on lean times, it will feel a severe shortage of good people in boom times, when other firms skim the cream from the market. On the other hand, if staff numbers are determined by the workload during peaks of activity, in quiet times the firm will have trouble finding enough work for all of them and will either have to retrench many of them or sustain significant operational losses.

One of the solutions to this dilemma is the formation of specialised, individual project-orientated consulting teams, which assemble for a specific assignment, finish it off and disassemble. That way firms can bring in the right talent and expertise to suit the assignment, as opposed to using in-house talent, which costs money to keep. Some call the whole principle 'outsourcing'.

Firms hire specialists on a limited time basis to work on their assignments, coordinate their actions and efforts and, hopefully, get much higher value for their money, which is a potential benefit for clients as well. However, more often than not, those benefits are not passed on to the clients, as profits are usually retained by the consulting firm.

Using consultants as business spies

I have bought Golden opinions from all sorts of people.
                                        Shakespeare, *Macbeth*

Management consultants quite often (usually unintentionally) play the role of business spy. They have the advantage of being able to do surveys and analyses and to ask detailed questions without arousing suspicion. Although companies investigated that way may suspect one of their competitors of pulling strings behind the scenes, they usually don't insist on finding out why questions are asked and who the client is.

Clients are generally isolated from their competitors' operations, their problems, plans and achievements. Consultants aren't. Clients are often brainwashed by their organisational cultures, inbred attitudes and limited paradigms, so they need to expand their horizons and learn about what their competitors and customers are doing.

Many managers have an uneasy feeling that they may be missing an important development somewhere else or that their competitors are doing certain things better. Consultants may help them get an insight into the hidden outside world. Whatever the case, a shrewd client can gain some very useful 'third party' information from consultants.

Consulting a small business

The future belongs to small business – lean, innovative, adaptive, customer-oriented, value-driven. For the past decade, many trends have been indicating the increasing importance of small enterprises.

Consulting, as a profession, focuses primarily on medium and large clients, but this doesn't mean that consultants aren't amongst those who are riding the current wave in small business entrepreneurship. After all, many small businesses have relatively big problems, which is the main reason why they either stay small or cease to exist.

What is so specific about consulting projects in small businesses? First of all, they are run by an individual or a small group of people. In many cases solving business problems really means solving personnel problems – training them, improving their knowledge, making them aware of their inadequacies and the ways to overcome those deficiencies. It may also mean resolving disputes or misunderstandings between partners or between the owner and the employees. Most consulting work with small businesses is therefore educational.

Due to their size and higher vulnerability, small businesses are very wary about the use of consultants. Most are concerned about the relatively high fees consultants charge and the lack of guarantee that desired results will be achieved. This is compounded by a tendency amongst some consultants to charge somewhat higher fees for short assignments and by their preference for longer ones, which may make smaller clients feel less wanted and less important (the 'second-class client' syndrome). Very rarely will consultants reduce their fees for small businesses. By doing that they would admit that the larger clients are overcharged.

Then there is the question of value for money. Many consultants who are used to projects and assignments with larger clients tend to 'overconsult' the small business. They stay too long on the job, engineer solutions that are too complex, too expensive and completely unnecessary. As a consequence, the small businessman doesn't get value for his money.

Furthermore, the nature and requirements of a typical small business assignment are usually different from those of a bigger client. Therefore, the consultant's experience, approach and methods have to match those requirements. What is needed in most cases is an integrated approach, which will improve the client's business as a whole, not just a certain aspect of it, as is the case with most projects with bigger clients.

A successful small-business consultant is less likely to be a distinguished specialist and more likely to be a well-experienced generalist, with working and practical knowledge of all relevant aspects of a small business venture. He must be able to think small and know what works on that scale and what doesn't. There are some consultants of that kind, all-rounders who know what small business needs and are able to provide inexpensive, fast and effective solutions to business problems.

If you are a small-business owner, don't deprive yourself and your enterprise of the benefits consulting could bring, and don't allow fears and preconceived notions to govern your attitudes towards consulting. Follow the basic steps outlined in this book, keep firmly focused on your ultimate goal and use every opportunity to talk to consultants and learn from them. Start with small projects, just to test the water. If the solutions work, count your blessings and keep using the winning tactics on bigger jobs. If they don't, regard the costs involved as a tuition fee for your continuous education and the cost of acquiring first-hand, real-life experience.

Conclusion

The golden rules of the consulting profession

> *One. Whenever anyone asks how long you've been in this business, you never say less than two years. Right. If a guy sees you don't know shit from shineola, he ain't gonna do what you want him to. Two. Never meet any of the client's people after work. Never accept lifts from them or drinks. Never talk about anything but work, never tell them anything about our business. We got competitors. We don't want no one knowin' what we're doin'. Three. Never screw the clients' women. No secretaries. Nothin'. We pay you to go home at weekends. You do your f**kin' there.*

These are Neil Martin's rules, from his hilarious novel, *The American Way*. What follows are more basic rules, on a more profound level, which, nevertheless, govern consultants' day-to-day behaviour.

1. Once in, never out.
2. Lose anything but clients.
3. Get paid.
4. The client is always right.
5. When the client is wrong, rule 4 applies.

The value paradox

Have you ever asked yourself why management seldom listens to ideas, proposals and suggestions made by employees, while it blindly follows those same ideas, proposals and suggestions when coming from consultants? The answer lies in the perceived value. In the first case, the advice is free. Employees volunteer the information and ideas. Managers don't have to pay for it and don't appreciate it. In the second case, which may be called 'you get what you pay for', the recipient of the service values and appreciates the knowledge, information or ideas, just because of the high price-tag that is attached to it.

Who gets the most out of consultants?

Well-found consultants can stay in a company for ever, moving from one divisional trouble spot to another like Arabs wandering from oasis to oasis.

Robert Heller, *The Naked Manager*

Consultants know that they do their best work with their best clients. Not only are they controlled, assisted and guided better, but the whole environment is more conducive to change, which is one of the benefits consultants are hired to bring in.

This simply means that the better-managed, more efficient and more innovative the client company is, the more it will get out of consultants. It also means that those companies who badly need consultants get the least out of them.

Alternatives

I don't like to hire consultants. They're like castrated bulls; all they can do is advise.

Victor Kiam, *Going For It!*

Corporations all over the world spend fortunes on consultants' fees. Armed with some basic knowledge, determination and a clear, logical approach, they could do many of the jobs themselves. Solutions can be found anywhere, sometimes in places where you least expect them to be found and from people you don't expect help from.

Eighty per cent of consulting assignments are pure and simple searches for common-sense solutions. These searches could easily be done by your own staff. Throw in a challenge, let people grow professionally and personally, and you'll be amazed at the number and quality of suggestions and solutions they'll come back with.

❑ Read magazines, newsletters, catalogues, product news, books and news releases which cover your areas of concern or interest.

❑ Attend seminars, workshops, conferences, symposiums, meetings which deal with issues of importance to you and which are attended by people who either share your problems or have solutions to them.

❑ Pay attention to your competitors. Observe what they do and listen to what they say about your company and your products or services. In many cases it will be more accurate and much cheaper than paying consultants to discover the same truths, let alone acting on your beliefs and self-perceptions, which is often a recipe for disaster.

❑ Talk to business contacts, friends, members of professional bodies or institutions, colleagues who may have been involved in a similar project or had a problem similar to yours. You can also learn from them about consulting projects they have had, about methods and strategies that work and those that don't. Establish a support group that will share experiences and provide back-up in times of trouble.

❑ Talk to people in your organisation. Brainstorm. Explore options and possibilities. Actively seek everybody's input and contribution. Provide an atmosphere conducive to free expression of opinions and concerns, let people come and talk to you about issues, problems and solutions.

Managing consultants – a multidisciplinary approach

Clients from various industries and with various backgrounds are still looking for a strategic framework which will synthesise methods, techniques and new developments into a logical, coherent system, enabling them to evaluate options and apply management methods to the art of managing consultants and to maximise the value of consultants' contributions to them and their companies. Managing consultants is quintessentially a behavioural science, although heavily influenced by legal, technical, financial and organisational factors.

The following list defines the major areas, disciplines and skills that relate to and form that unique and specific management discipline – managing consultants:

❑ Project management (techniques, forms, scheduling, monitoring, control, computer tools)
❑ Quality control (accreditation, standards, specification, compliance)
❑ Effective communication (verbal, listening, speed reading, writing, presentation skills)
❑ Accounting (budgeting, forecasting, justifications, cost control, feasibility studies)
❑ Personnel management (selecting consultants, performance evaluation, guidance, counselling)
❑ Contract law and other legal issues (obligations, laws, regulations, contracts, disputes, liabilities)
❑ General management and business skills (motivation, supervision, negotiating)

CLIENT'S STRATEGIES

DIAGNOSTIC
1. DATA GATHERING
2. FACT FINDING
3. OBSERVATION
4. SURVEYS AND INTERVIEWS
5. INVESTIGATIONS
6. EVALUATING OPTIONS, SOLUTIONS AND INFORMATION

SOCIAL
1. BUILDING EFFECTIVE CLIENT - CONSULTANT RELATIONSHIPS
2. COMMUNICATION
3. TEAM BUILDING
4. LEARNING

TECHNO - STRUCTURAL
1. IMPLEMENTING CHANGE
2. REDESIGN OF EQUIPMENT AND SYSTEMS
3. INTRODUCING OR MODIFYING PROCEDURES, RULES, STANDARDS
4. PUTTING RECOMMENDATIONS INTO PRACTICE

OPERATIONAL
1. METHODS TO BE USED
2. FORMAL PROCEDURES RULES AND REQUIREMENTS

GOALS

Consulting – a role model for the future?

Some management gurus, such as Tom Peters, the former McKinsey & Co. consultant and author of *In Search of Excellence*, believe that consultancies are the role models for the organisations of the future. Consultancies employ 'knowledge workers' and trade that knowledge for profit. They function as cross-functional project teams, loosely linked groups of people who market their services, create projects and challenge the status quo.

The consulting profession is anything but static. It is continuing to mature and evolve. New techniques, methods, concepts and operational philosophies are bringing much-needed change to archaic relationships, value systems and the way consultancies operate.

Failure and success

> Success is the continuous journey towards the achievement of predetermined, worthwhile goals.

> Tom Hopkins

Mental exercise	
From which of the two lists can you remember more things?	
List A	List B
Teamwork	Blame
Motivation	Litigation
Challenge	Disputes
Professionalism	Intimidation
Dedication	Variations

If you open any self-improvement book, be it by Anthony Robbins, Dale Carnegie or Tom Hopkins, the common claim is that the thread that links the winners in life is their refusal to accept failure and their ability to deal with success. The losers are the opposite. They accept failure easily and learn to live with it, while not being able to cope with success. The mental paradigms of our minds are somehow ill-prepared for success; we pre-programme ourselves for failure. And we always become what we think – if you think your project will fail, it will. If you believe in its success, it will succeed. Either way, you'll prove yourself correct.

The Psychological Aspects of Failure and Success in Consulting
- ❏ The failure syndrome in consulting is based on the failure of both clients and consultants to recognise and accept the fact that failures are a direct consequence of the inexperience of one or both parties.
- ❏ The success syndrome is based on the inability to recognise what actions and qualities led to success and the inability to deal with that success.
- ❏ Both clients and consultants have difficulties in accepting either failure or success. Failure, interestingly enough, is much easier accepted than success is!

Success is a result of continuous improvement. Don't expect sudden gains and breakthroughs. Success is a journey, not a jump. Consistent, systematic and gradual improvement is the foundation stone for management success. Numerous studies have shown that humans, on average, use only about twenty per cent of their abilities. Very poor, don't you think? With that in view, do you think you can make a hundred per cent improvement your goal?

Of course you can. But there is a catch: don't go for a hundred per cent improvement in any one thing. Aim to achieve a one per cent better performance in one hundred things. One per cent doesn't seem much, but it can make a big difference.

Five per cent commission
Two school friends met each other after twenty years. One graduated top of his class in a business school and worked as a management consultant for a small marketing and advertising firm. The other, who never showed any signs of intelligence and achievement, formed his own trading company and became a millionaire.

'How did you manage to build such a profitable venture for yourself?' asked the consultant.

'It's all pretty simple. You see, I've got a couple of products that I buy for five dollars and sell for ten dollars. You wouldn't believe how much money can be made on a five per cent mark-up.'

The ten commandments for handling consultants
1.   Employ them on quality, not on price.
2.   Let them know your expectations.
3.   Stay close to them.

4. Practise common sense.
5. Measure and control.
6. Communicate regularly.
7. Monitor their progress.
8. Take corrective action promptly.
9. Learn in the process.
10. Make them make you look good.

At the end

Page by page, point by point, we have reached the end of our journey together. I hope that our voyage through consulting waters was not only interesting, but also beneficial. I would like to think that you'll adopt and apply some of the outlined principles in your own dealings with consultants, and make both your company and the client–consultant business in general more efficient and prosperous.

The last point I would like to make is that no matter how much you talk to other users of consulting services or consultants themselves, no matter how many books dealing with consulting or business topics you read, you won't get very far without actually managing consulting projects yourself. No one can do it for you and no one can learn without making certain mistakes himself.

A matter of feedback

Writing a book that can serve as a universal guide to clients from various backgrounds and professions is not an easy task. There is always some room for improvement and some important things that get overlooked. As happens in life, you may not agree with everything I say. The main purpose of this book is to start you thinking about consultants and to give you a foundation for your own ideas, methods and tactics.

If you have something to say about it please do so. Write to me. I hope your suggestions, comments and criticism will help me to make future editions of this book better and more beneficial to readers.

Further Reading

Albert, K.J., *How to Solve Business Problems,* New York: McGraw-Hill (1983)

Bell, C.R. and Nader, L. (ed.), *The Client–Consultant Handbook,* Houston: Gulf Publishing Company (1979)

Bermont, H., *How to Become a Successful Consultant In Your Own Field,* St Martin's Press (1991)

Holtz, H., *How To Succeed As an Independent Consultant,* New York: John Wiley & Sons, Inc. (1983)

Karlson, D., *Marketing Your Consulting and Professional Services,* Menlo Park: Crisp (1988)

Lock, D., *Project Management,* Aldershot: Gower (1992)

Ogilvy, D., *Confessions of an Advertising Man,* New York: Ballantine Books (1963)

Sveiby, K.E. and Lloyd, T., *Managing Knowhow,* London: Bloomsbury (1988)

Tepper, R., *Consultant's Proposal, Fee, and Contract Problem Solver,* New York: John Wiley & Sons, Inc. (1993)

Ucko, T., *Selecting and Working With Consultants,* Menlo Park: Crisp (1990)

Index